ST. BASIL THE GREAT
ON THE HOLY SPIRIT

ST. BASIL THE GREAT ON THE HOLY SPIRIT

ST. VLADIMIR'S SEMINARY PRESS
CRESTWOOD, NEW YORK 10707
1980

Library of Congress Cataloging in Publication Data

Basilius, Saint, the Great, Abp. of Caesarea, 330
  (ca.)-379.
  On the Holy Spirit.

Includes bibliographical references.
    1. Holy Spirit—Early works to 1800. I. Anderson,
David, 1953-   II. Title.
BT120.B313   231'.3   80-25502
ISBN 0-913836-74-5

Translation © 1980
St. Vladimir's Seminary Press
575 Scarsdale Road
Crestwood, New York 10707

ISBN 0-913836-74-5

PRINTED IN THE UNITED STATES OF AMERICA
BY
ATHENS PRINTING COMPANY
NEW YORK, NY

TABLE OF CONTENTS

INTRODUCTION

"We believe in the Holy Spirit, the Lord, the Giver of Life, who proceeds from the Father; who with the Father and the Son together is worshipped and glorified." So states the creed employed by the fathers who met in Constantinople in 381. Half a century earlier, at Nicaea in 325, the Holy Spirit had been mentioned almost as an afterthought: "We believe in the Holy Spirit," the original Nicene creed simply stated, and that was all. But fifty storm-tossed years between the two councils proved that such vagueness would not do, that the Church of Christ was disintegrating into a jumble of warring factions, and that Θεοπρεπεῖς λόγοι, words adequate for God, were necessary to define the catholic faith. As St. Basil wrote this treatise from his episcopal city of Caesarea at the request of his spiritual son Bishop Amphilochios of Iconium, he could only compare the state of the Church to a naval battle being fought in the midst of a raging tempest, in which the two fleets are so broken up by the storm that banners can no longer be seen, signals are no longer recognized, and one cannot distinguish one's ally from one's foe. Perhaps the first thing the modern reader should recognize concerning this book is that despite its polished rhetoric and elaborately-constructed syllogisms, it is essentially a treatise written *in tempore belli*; St. Basil is using his talents to help steer the Church away from imminent shipwreck.

It was of course the Arian controversy that was causing such havoc in the Church; and it is important not to oversimplify this conflict into a clear-cut battle between those who believed that Jesus was God and those who did not. A study of the conflict reveals four basic "groups": the "old" Nicaeans, who insisted that the Nicene Creed's declaration that the Son is of one essence (*homoousios*) with the Father must be upheld to the extent that acceptance of the word *homoousios* was the only sure proof of orthodoxy. The "new" Nicaeans, including St. Basil and the other Cappadocian fathers, although they unquestionably confessed Christ to be divine, thought that the use of *homoousios* could be ambiguous (*of one essence* could be misconstrued to mean that the Son and the Father were the same person), and for a time they preferred to use the term *homoiousios*, meaning that the Son is of a *like* or *similar* essence with the Father. These "old" and "new" Nicaeans by and large came to realize that they professed the same faith; their difficulty lay in resolving which word was the most acceptable. But saying that the Son was *like* the Father had its own ambiguities; for to what *extent* was He like the Father? There were those who accepted the use of *homoiousios*, but nevertheless stressed the differences between Father and Son so much that if the divinity of the Son was not denied, it certainly was not affirmed very strongly; these may be called the semi-Arians. Then there were the radical Arians, those who placed the Son in the created order, denying that He was similar or equal to the Father in any way. In the midst of all this confusion another problem raised its head: what about the Holy Spirit, concerning whom relatively little is said in Scripture? Those who denied the divinity of Christ were not about to affirm the divinity of the Spirit, but the radical Arians were fast becoming a small minority. Most others did not know what to think; they knew they had been baptized in the name of Father, Son, and Spirit; they sang hymns praising the three persons; they understood that by the outpouring of the Spirit on Pentecost the proclamation of the saving Gospel to the ends of the world was made possible. But the question of what sort of being the Holy Spirit was simply had not been answered; one only has to read this treatise to discover the variety of opinions popular at the time. Arianizing elements felt that by fighting against the doctrine of the Holy Spirit's divinity (thus earning for themselves the name *Pneumatomachoi*, or fighters against the Spirit) they would succeed in undermining Nicene orthodoxy. But St. Basil realized that by writing a book affirming the equality of the Spirit with the Father and the Son, he could make a water-tight case for orthodoxy: if we are bound to confess the divinity of the Spirit, we must confess the Trinity to be three persons sharing the same divine nature; once this is accomplished, it is much easier to determine what is orthodoxy and what is not. So his primary objective in this treatise is to clear up the muddle — a muddle which he denounces as the end-product of vanity and pride, caused by those who dare to utter clever-sounding words about God without loving truth in their hearts, who refuse to measure their own opinions with the yardstick of the Church's living faith, who admit of no absolute standard outside themselves. He writes during a time when persecutions are past, when Christianity is becoming fashionable, a "state" religion subject to the whims of emperors influenced by ambitious ecclesiastics. His struggle is one for truth, the changeless truth which the Lord promised would bring freedom to those who know it, and in possession of which men would be enabled to fulfill their destiny to become like God, to become by grace what God is by nature.

St. Basil was educated in the schools of Athens, which at his time were still flourishing. He received thorough training in the classical disciplines of rhetoric and logic, and then placed his formidable intelligence in the service of the Church. He treats his subject with an exhaustiveness which may easily weary the modern reader, but which is

necessary for the inductive process to be successful: the
more specific the evidence, the more definite the conclusion.
Many readers might be perplexed or even scandalized when
they discover that nowhere in the entire treatise does
St. Basil bluntly say: "the Holy Spirit is God" or "God
the Holy Spirit," but it must be borne in mind that such
a statement is nowhere to be found in Scripture. This ex-
plains why St. Basil and the other Cappadocian fathers
are unwilling to make a *general* statement of the Holy
Spirit's divinity; instead, they prefer to assemble all the
witnesses available in Scripture and in the baptismal and
liturgical tradition of the Church, and when they have
examined all the evidence, they unmistakably conclude
that the Spirit indeed is divine (avoiding, even in their
conclusions, the use of "untraditional" general statements).
Thus, although one will never read that "the Holy Spirit
is God" in St. Basil's treatise, one will find numerous statements that "the Holy Spirit partakes of the fullness of
divinity" (see paragraph 46). This is not rhetorical hair-
splitting; rather, it reveals a great pastoral wisdom: present
all the evidence so that confession of the Spirit's divinity
is the only possible orthodox choice, but avoid, at a time
when unspiritual men yearn to multiply controversies, the
use of an unprecedented statement.

Much of St. Basil's argument consists in showing that
we can tell who the Spirit *is* by examining what He *does*.
He is called the *Holy* Spirit, and because of His holiness
creatures are made holy. The holiness of a creature cannot
sanctify other creatures; only someone who is holy by
nature can sanctify. Since only God is holy by nature, and
since according to the Scripture it is the Holy Spirit who
sanctifies men, then the Holy Spirit must be divine. The
other operations of the Spirit are discussed in the same
logical way: it is the Spirit who renews the face of the
earth; the gifts of the Spirit cause "knowledge of the future,
understanding of mysteries, heavenly citizenship, endless

joy in the presence of God, becoming like God, and the highest of all desires, becoming God" (paragraph 23). How could a creature be the origin of such blessings? If Scripture says that "no one can say 'Jesus is Lord' except by the Holy Spirit" (I Cor. 12:3), how can a creature be the inspiration by which the saving Gospel is proclaimed? To reject the divinity of the Holy Spirit is to reject His work of sanctification and His gifts of faith and renewal, and thus is a rejection of salvation itself. If saving regeneration begins through baptism in the name of Father, Son, and Spirit, with *name* in the singular, then Father, Son, and Spirit form a coordinate series, with all three sharing equal rank. Finally, if baptism must be administered in the name of Father, Son, and Spirit, then praise, thanksgiving, and worship must be offered in the same way. *Lex orandi lex est credendi*; worship must use the same terms as the profession of faith.

The question of exactly how glory was to be ascribed to God is the cause of the lengthy grammatical discussions in this treatise which surely bring frustration to reader and translator alike. The problem was this: St. Basil was attacked for using the form "Glory to the Father with (μετά) the Son together with (σύν) the Holy Spirit" in his church. The customary form for the Greek-speaking churches at the time was "Glory to the Father through (διά) the Son in (ἐν) the Holy Spirit," although as St. Basil points out, the first formula had long been traditional in many of the non-Greek-speaking churches of the East. At Caesarea Basil used both formulas; he thought that the first formula was best for adoration offered to the Godhead, while the second was most appropriate for describing the way God deals with man. Thus he recognized that two sets of theological terminology are necessary: one to describe God as God, and another to describe God's plan of salvation for men. Although no contradiction can be involved, different words are often necessary for the sake of precision. In order to demonstrate that there was no conflict between the two doxologies, he first had to prove that the prepositions *through* and *in* do not subordinate the persons of Son and Spirit, as his opponents claimed. He accomplishes this by enumerating dozens of Scriptural texts in which these very prepositions are used in reference to the Father, and accuses the Pneumato-machoi of imitating the vocabulary of pagan philosophy instead of Scripture. His next task is to justify the use of *with*, which is not found in Scripture, since the baptismal formula of Mt. 28:19 uses *and*. Here St. Basil appeals to common sense: in everyday speech there is no real differ-ence between *and* and *with*. Although one is a conjunction and one a preposition, they serve the same purpose; the only possible difference is that in a series of names *with* implies co-operation better than *and*. Since it is abundantly clear from Scripture that Father, Son, and Holy Spirit cooperate, how can anyone denounce the use of *with?* Here St. Basil offers his opponents a compromise: if they utterly refuse to use *with the Spirit* because it cannot be found in Scripture, he will settle for everyone using *and,* which adequately expresses unity of the persons in one nature. This was certainly a prophetic compromise, since that is the form of the doxology which finally was adopted by all catholic Christians.

It is this translator's opinion that a good dose of dry, logical Cappadocian theology can serve as an effective antidote for the subjective emotionalism in which modern Christians frequently find themselves engulfed. Doctrine these days is often ignored, taken for granted or replaced with individualism, and perhaps the fathers can help us by reminding us (often in many words!) that God be-came man to show us the truth which gives life and freedom, a truth which is eternal. This is the principal reason for attempting a modern English translation of this book, the only previous translation being done in the last century by Rev. Blonfield Jackson, presently found in Volume 8 of the Nicene and Post-Nicene Fathers series. This translation is a complete revision of the former; the Greek text used was that found in Volume 32 of Migne's *Patrologia Graeca.* May the Lord who is the Spirit, through the prayers of St. Basil, enlighten us with the knowledge that inspired the fathers who have gone before us, that we may be led to the vision of the glory of God, shining in the face of Christ.

DAVID ANDERSON
August 1980

CHAPTER 1. *Introductory comment concerning the necessity of examining even the smallest theological questions.*

1. My well-beloved and most honorable brother Amphilochios: I applaud your love of learning and your diligence in study. Indeed, I am amazed by the care and sobriety of your thoughts, particularly when you say that none of the words used to describe God should be passed over without exact examination, no matter what their context. You have profited from the Lord's exhortation, "Every one who asks, receives, and he who seeks, finds." [1] It seems to me that your eagerness to learn would move even those who are reluctant to share what they know. But what I admire most about you is that your questions reflect a sincere desire to discover the truth, not like many these days who ask questions only to test others. There is certainly no lack nowadays of people who delight in asking endless questions just to have something to babble about, but it is difficult to find someone who loves truth in his soul, who seeks the truth as medicine for his ignorance. Just as the hunter hides his traps, or an ambush of soldiers camouflages itself, so these questioners spew forth elaborately constructed inquiries, not really hoping to learn anything useful from them, because unless you agree with them and give them the answer they want, they imagine that they are fully entitled to stir up a raging controversy.

2. But if "Wisdom shall be given to a fool who seeks after wisdom," [2] how great is the price at which we should

---

[1] Lk. 11:10.   [2] Prov. 17:28 (LXX).

value the "wise hearer," whom the Prophet places in the
company of the "honorable counselor"? [3] He first deserves
to be given a hearty welcome, but then he should be urged
on in the company of those who share his zeal, who labor
with him in all things, as he presses forward to perfection.
Those who are idle in the pursuit of righteousness count
theological terminology as secondary, together with attempts to search out the hidden meaning in this phrase or
that syllable, but those conscious of the goal of our calling
realize that we are to become like God, as far as this is
possible for human nature. But we cannot become like
God unless we have knowledge of Him, and without lessons there will be no knowledge. Instruction begins with
the proper use of speech, and syllables and words are the
elements of speech. Therefore to scrutinize syllables is not
a superfluous task. Just because certain questions seem insignificant is no reason to ignore them. Hunting truth is no
easy task; we must look everywhere for its tracks. Learning truth is like learning a trade; apprentices grow in experience little by little, provided they do not despise any
opportunity to increase their knowledge. If a man spurns
fundamental elements as insignificant trifles, he will never
embrace the fullness of wisdom. "Yes" and "No" are only
two syllables, yet truth, the best of all good things, as well
as falsehood, the worst possible evil, are most often expressed by these two small words. Why do I mention this?
Because in former times someone on trial could join the
ranks of Christ's martyrs by a single nod of his head, for
this one act signified total commitment to true religion.
If this is so, what theological term is so insignificant that
it will not greatly upset the balance of the scales, unless it
is used correctly? We are told that "not one jot nor one
tittle shall pass away from the law;" [4] how then could we
safely pass by even the smallest point? The questions that

---

[3] Cf. Is. 3:3 (LXX).   [4] Mt. 5:18.

you want us to examine are both small and great: small, because it only takes a moment to utter the words in question — and for this reason they are thought to be negligible — but the force of their meaning is great. They can be compared to the mustard seed, for it is the smallest of all seeds, but when properly grown its potential is revealed; it is the greatest of shrubs and becomes a tree.[5] Anyone who laughs at the subtlety of our use of syllables, while at the same time craftily devising false subtleties of his own, as the Psalmist says,[6] will end up reaping laughter's barren fruit. But as for us, let us not succumb to the reproaches of men, or be conquered by their contempt, so that we abandon our investigation. Far be it from me to be ashamed of these small matters; indeed, if I ever attain to even a fraction of their dignity, I would congratulate both myself for having won great honor and my brother and fellow-investigator for an achievement far above the mediocre. I am aware that little words express a great controversy, and in hope of winning the prize I will not hesitate to work. I am convinced that this discussion will prove to be useful for me, and fruitful for my hearers. Therefore, I begin this explanation asking the Holy Spirit to enlighten me, and with your approval, in order to point out the direction that the discussion will take, I will return for a moment to the origin of our question.

3. Lately while I pray with the people, we sometimes finish the doxology to God the Father with the form "Glory to the Father *with* the Son, *together with* the Holy Spirit," and at other times we use "Glory to the Father *through* the Son *in* the Holy Spirit." Some of those present accused us of using strange and mutually contradictory terms. But your wish certainly is to help these people, or, if they should prove completely incurable, to safeguard

---

[5] Cf. Mt. 13:31-32.   [6] Ps. 119:85 (LXX).

those who associate with them; that is why you think that clear teaching concerning the force underlying these prepositions is desirable. I will write as concisely as possible, hoping to present a suitable beginning for this discussion.

CHAPTER 2. *The origin of the way heretics closely observe the use of prepositions.*

4. Someone aware of the importance of small matters might suppose the meticulousness of these men with syllables and words reflects straightforwardness. Such is not the case, however; for no small evil is risked here, but a deep and hidden plot against true religion. Their contention is that any mention of Father, Son, and Holy Spirit as dissimilar makes it easy to demonstrate that they are different in nature. They have an old trick invented by Aetius, the champion of this heresy, who writes in one of his letters that things whose natures are dissimilar are expressed in dissimilar terms, and, vice-versa, dissimilar terms are used to describe things whose natures are dissimilar. In his attempt to prove this he even drags in the Apostle's words: "one God and Father, *from* Whom are all things . . . and one Lord Jesus Christ, *through* Whom are all things." [7] He then goes on to say that the relationship between these prepositions (*from* and *through*) indicates the relationship between the *natures* they describe, and, since the expression "from whom" differs from "through whom," the Father is therefore different from the Son. This pestilence of a heresy depends entirely upon the subtleties of these men concerning the above prepositons. They assign the words "from whom" to God

---

[7] I Cor. 8:6.

the Father as if this expression was His one special allotment; for God the Son they select the phrase "through whom," and for the Holy Spirit "in which," and they say that this assignment of prepositions must never be interchanged, in order that, as I have already said, one prepositional phrase is always made to indicate a corresponding nature. It is obvious that by quibbling over prepositions they try to maintain the force of their impious argument. By the expression "from whom" they wish to indicate the Creator; by "through whom" they mean an instrument of service, and "in which" they use to refer to time or place. The holy Creator of all things is thus made into a mere instrument, and the Holy Spirit appears to furnish creation with nothing except time and place.

CHAPTER 3. *How technical discussion of prepositions originated in pagan philosophy.*

5. They have been led into this error, however, by their study of pagan writers, who apply the expressions "from whom" and "through whom" to things which are by nature distinct. These writers suppose that "from whom" refers to the matter from which something is made,[8] and "through whom" to the instrument which assists in its making. In addition to this (for a moment let us consider their entire argument, in order to expose its incompatibility with the truth and its inconsistency with their own teaching) those who study this vain philosophy, while they discuss

---

[8] St. Basil here refers to the four Aristotelian causes: formal, material, efficient, and final. (See the *Posterior Analytics*, Book 2, Ch. 11).

the many aspects of causality and attempt to appropriately categorize them, say that some causes are initial, some are co-operative or contributory, while others are indispensable. For each of these they use a separate preposition, so that the maker is referred to in one way, and the instrument in another. They say that the expression most suitable for the maker is "by whom;" for example, the chair is always produced *by* the carpenter. The instrument is described as the thing "through which" something is made; e.g. the chair is made "through" or "by means of" certain tools: the axe, the drill, etc. "*From* which" refers to the material used, which, in this case, is wood, while "*according* to which" is understood to mean the pattern followed by the workman, since he either predetermines a mental sketch and then uses his imagination, or else guides his work with a visible pattern already provided for him. "*Because* of which," or "for the *sake* of which" they want to mean purpose or reason for existence; thus the chair exists for the sake of men. "*In* which" indicates time and place. When was it made? In this age. Where? In this place. Time and place might seem to contribute nothing to what is being produced, but outside them it would be impossible to make anything, since things are caused within the framework of place and time. Our opponents have first studied and admired these vain and empty distinctions, and then transferred them to the simple and uncluttered doctrine of the Spirit, using them to belittle God the Word and to deny the divine Spirit. Pagan philosophers reserved the phrase "*through* or *by means of* which" to refer to lifeless tools or the most abject work, but now Christians bind the Master of all with prepositions, and are not ashamed to describe the Creator of the universe with language fit for a hammer or a saw.

CHAPTER 4. *How such a use of prepositions cannot be observed in Scripture.*

6. Now we admit that the Word of truth often uses these expressions in the manner just described, but we absolutely deny that the freedom of the Spirit is controlled by pagan pettiness. Rather, it appropriately varies its expressions for each occasion, as the circumstances require. For instance, *"from whom"* or *"from which"* does not *always* refer to matter, as pagan philosophy teaches, but Scripture is more likely to apply this phrase to the supreme cause: "one God, *from* Whom are all things" [9] or "all things are *from God*." [10] However, the word of truth often uses this same preposition when referring to matter; for example, it says, "You shall make an ark *from* incorruptible wood" [11] and "You shall make a lampstand *from* pure gold," [12] and "the first man was *from* the earth, a man of dust" [13] and "You are formed *from* the clay, as I am." [14] But our opponents, as we have already said, have decreed that this phrase concerns the Father alone, in order to prove their heresy of different natures. The source of this distinction of theirs is pagan philosophy, but they do not always precisely follow the system. They say *"in the Spirit"* and *"through"* the Son, and since they impose the title "instrument" on the Son, and "place" on the Spirit, here they are in comformity with their teachers. But when they apply "from Whom" to God (the Father) they no longer imitate the pagans, but claim that they have changed to apostolic usage, as it is written, *"from* Him is the source of your life in Christ Jesus" [15] and "all things are *from*

---

[9] I Cor. 8:6.　　　[12] Ex. 25:31.　　　[14] Job 33:6.
[10] I Cor. 11:12.　　[13] I Cor. 15:47.　　[15] Cf. I Cor. 1:30.
[11] Ex. 25:10.

God." [16] What is the result of this technical discussion? Cause has one nature, an instrument has another, and place yet another. So the Son's nature is alien to the Father's, since the tool is by nature different from the craftsman, and the nature of the Spirit is foreign to both, since place and time are different from tools or those who handle them.

CHAPTER 5. *How "through whom" is also said concerning the Father, and "from whom" for the Son and the Spirit.*

7. Having described our opponents' arguments, we shall now demonstrate our proposal: namely, that the Father does not accept "*from* whom" exclusively, and abandon "*through* whom" to the Son. Furthermore, we reject their arbitrary principle that the Son does not admit the Holy Spirit to share "*from* whom" or "*through* whom". "There is one God, the Father, *from* whom are all things . . . and one Lord Jesus Christ *through* whom are all things." [17] St. Paul does not say this to lay down an arbitrary law of prepositions, but to distinguish between the persons. He writes this not to introduce any division of natures, but to prove that the union of Father and Son is without confusion. It is obvious that the phrases in this passage do not contradict each other, nor do they separate the natures to which they are applied, like army squadrons facing each other in battle. The blessed Paul unites both for the same purpose when he says, "for *from* him and *through* him and *to* him are all things." [18] Even someone not paying much attention to the meaning of the words would admit that

---

[16] I Cor. 11:12.   [17] I Cor. 8:6.   [18] Rom. 11:36.

this passage clearly refers to the Lord. The Apostle has just quoted the prophecy of Isaiah: "Who has known the mind of the Lord, or who has been His counsellor," [19] and then goes on to say that "for from Him and through Him and to Him are all things." The prophet is speaking about God the Word, the Maker of all creation; we learn this from his previous words, "Who has measured the waters in the hollow of His hand and marked off the heavens with a span, enclosed the dust of the earth in a measure, and weighed the mountains in scales and the hills in a balance? Who has known the mind of the Lord or who has been His counsellor?" [20] This passage is not merely a rhetorical question; if it were, "who" could not possibly refer to anyone. Rather, the use of "who" indicates a rare personage. The following passages ask the same: "Who will rise up for me against the evildoers?" [21] or "What man is there who desires life," [22] or "Who shall ascend the hill of the Lord?" [23] All these questions, including "Who has known the mind of the Lord, or who has been His counsellor?" have the same answer: "For the Father loves the Son, and shows Him all that He Himself is doing." [24] He it is who holds the earth, grasping it with His hands. He has arranged all things in order; He set the mountains in their places and measured the waters. He assigns to each thing in the universe its proper rank. He encompasses the expanse of the heavens with only a small portion of His power, which the prophet in his oracle calls a span. The Apostle's words are well spoken: "For from Him and through Him and to Him are all things." [25] The cause of being comes *from* Him to all things that exist, according to the will of God the Father. *Through* Him structure and preservation are given to all things, for He created everything, and dispenses

---

[19] Is. 40:13; Rom. 12:34.

[20] Is. 40:12-13. [22] Ps. 34:12. [24] Jn. 5:20.

[21] Ps. 94:16. [23] Ps. 24:3. [25] Rom. 11:36.

well-being to all things, according to the need of each. Therefore all things are turned toward Him, looking with irresistible longing and unspeakable love to the creator and sustainer of life as it is written: "The eyes of all look hopefully to Thee," [26] and "These all look to Thee, to give them their food in due season," [27] and again, "Thou openest Thy hand, and satisfiest the desire of every living thing." [28]

8. If our opponents reject this interpretation, what argument will deliver them from openly falling into their own trap? If they will not permit these three expressions "from whom," "through whom" and "in whom" to be spoken concerning the Lord, they will be forced against their will to apply them to God the Father. Here their argument crumbles, because we find not only "from whom" but also "through whom" applied to the Father. "Through whom" indicates nothing derogatory; why in the world should it be used to confine the Son in an inferior position? If it always denotes subservience, let them explain to us to what superior the God of glory and the Father of Christ is subject. Truly they have overthrown themselves, while we are victorious on both sides. If the words "from Him and through Him and to Him are all things" refer to the Son, the *"from* Him" is discovered to be applied to the Son. On the other hand, if they contend that the words belong to the Father, then "through whom" is given to God (the Father) as His due. Both phrases have equal value, since both are used to describe God in the same way. Either the passage refers to the Father or the Son, and both prepositions describe either one Person, or the other; But let us return to our original topic.

9. Paul says in his epistle to the Ephesians: "Rather, speaking the truth in love, we are to grow up in every way

---

[26] Ps. 145:15.   [27] Ps. 104:27.   [28] Ps. 145:16.

into Him who is the head, into Christ, from whom the whole body, joined and knit together by every joint with which it is supplied, when each part is working properly, makes bodily growth and upbuilds itself in love." [29] Again in the epistle to the Colossians he says to those who have no understanding of the Only-Begotten, that ". . . not holding fast to the Head (that is, Christ) from whom the whole body, nourished and knit together through its joints and ligaments, grows with a growth that is from God." [30] From another passage we learn that Christ is the head of the Church, as the Apostle says: "He has made Him the head over all things for the Church," [31] and, "from His fulness we have all received." [32] The Lord Himself says: "He will take what is mine and declare it to you." [33] The industrious reader will notice that the phrase "from whom" is used in many different ways. For instance, the Lord says, "I perceive that power has gone forth from me." [34] Similarly we observe that "from whom" is frequently used in reference to the Spirit. Paul says: "He who sows to the Spirit will reap eternal life *from* the Spirit." [35] John writes: "And by this we know that He abides in us, *from* the Spirit which He has given us." [36] The angel says to Joseph: "that which is conceived in her is *from* the Holy Spirit." [37] The Lord says: "That which is born *from* the Spirit is spirit." [38] Such is the case so far.

10. We must now demonstrate that the phrase "through whom" or "by whom" is used by Scripture to refer to Father, Son, and Holy Spirit alike. As far as the Son is concerned, we will not enumerate the multitude of references available, for they are well-known, and our op-

---

[29] Eph. 4:15-16.   [33] Jn. 16:15.   [36] I Jn. 3:24.
[30] Col. 2:19.   [34] Lk. 8:46.   [37] Lk. 1:20.
[31] Eph. 1:22.   [35] Gal. 6:8.   [38] Jn. 3:6.
[32] Jn. 1:16.

ponents build their argument by using them. We will show,
however, that "through whom" or "by whom" is used in
reference to the Father. It is written: "God is faithful,
through whom you were called into the fellowship of His
Son, Jesus Christ our Lord." [39] and "Paul, an apostle of
Christ Jesus *by* the will of God" [40] and again, "So *through*
God you are no longer a slave but a son, and if a son
then an heir," [41] and "so that as Christ was raised from
the dead *by* the glory of the Father ..." [42] Isaiah says:
"Woe to them that take secret counsel, and not *by* the
Lord." [43] This same phrase is used many times to refer
to the Spirit as well: "Guard the truth that has been entrusted to you *by* the Holy Spirit," [44] and it says in another
place, "To one is given *through* the Spirit the utterance of
wisdom." [45]

11. We can say the same concerning the preposition
in; Scripture uses it to refer to God the Father. In the Old
Testament it says, that "*in* God we shall do valiantly" [46]
and "Blessed are the people ... who exult *in* Thy name
all the day." [47] Paul says, ". . . *in* God Who created all
things" and "Paul and Timothy, to the church of the
Thessalonians *in* God our Father" [48] and "asking that some-
how *in* God's will I may now at last succeed in coming to
you" [49] and "make your boast *in* God.[50] The rest are too
numerous to be mentioned; we do not wish to accumulate
evidence for its own sake, but to prove that our opponents'
opinions are unsound. Therefore I will not enumerate the
instances where the preposition "in" is used to describe the
Lord and the Holy Spirit, because they are so widespread.
But I cannot refrain from remarking that the "wise hearer"
may easily discover that if terminological differences in-

---

[39] I Cor. 1:9.   [43] Is. 29:15.   [47] Ps. 89:16.
[40] II Cor. 1:1.   [44] II Tim. 1:14.   [48] II Thess. 1:1.
[41] Gal. 4:7.   [45] I Cor. 12:8.   [49] Rom. 1:10.
[42] Rom. 6:4.   [46] Ps. 108:13.   [50] Rom. 2:17.

dicate differences in nature, then our opponents must shamefully agree that identical terminology is used for identical natures. Thus ample proof of our proposition has been provided.

12. The use of the above prepositions not only varies in discussions concerning the divine nature, but the meanings of the prepositions themselves are often interchangeable and are transferred from one subject to the other. For instance, Adam says "I have gained a man *through* God" [51] which means the same as *from* God. It says in another passage, "Moses charged . . . Israel *through* the commandment of the Lord," [52] and again, "Is not the interpretation . . . *through* God?" [53] Joseph, when he spoke to his fellow-prisoners concerning dreams, instead of saying *from* God, plainly says *through* God. Sometimes Paul does just the opposite: he uses "*from* whom" instead of "*through* whom"; for example, in the passage "born *from* woman" [54] instead of "through woman," but in another place he clearly distinguishes between these two prepositions when he says that woman is made *from* man, but man is born *through* woman: "As woman was made *from* man, so man is now born *of* (*through*) woman" [55] But in these same passages, where Paul demonstrates that these terms are used in different ways, he also corrects the error of those who imagine that the Lord's body is not a material body: He says that the Lord was born *from* woman to show that the God-bearing flesh was formed from the common stuff of humanity. If he had said that the Lord was born *through* woman someone might suspect that woman is merely the passive means of generation, but by saying that Christ was born *from* (the) woman he satisfactorily shows that the mother and her offspring share

---

[51] Gen. 4:1.   [53] Gen. 40:8.   [55] I Cor. 11:12.
[52] Num. 36:1.   [54] Gal. 4:4.

communion of natures. Paul in no way contradicts himself, but shows that these words can easily be interchanged. *From whom* and *through whom* are used interchangeably for the same subjects, depending on the context of the passage, so how can anyone say that the phrases can be invariably distinguished from each other, falsely attempting to find fault with true religion?

CHAPTER 6. *He disputes with those who assert that the Son is not with, but after the Father. Also concerning the equal glory of the Father and the Son.*

13.   Our opponents, who attempt to defeat our argument with subtle technicalities, cannot even take refuge in pleading ignorance. Obviously they object because we finish the doxology by giving glory to the Father *with* the Only-begotten One, and do not exclude the Holy Spirit from this same glory. Because of this they call us innovators, revolutionaries, phrase-coiners, and who knows how many other insults. But I am so far from being unable to endure their abuse that, were it not for the fact that their loss causes me tears and continual sorrow, I could almost thank them for their blasphemy, because through them I have obtained a blessing. The Lord says, "Blessed are you when men shall revile you ... for my sake." [56] These are the reasons for their vexation: they say that the Son is not equal with the Father, but comes after the Father. Therefore it follows that glory should be ascribed to the Father *through* Him, but not *with* Him. *With* Him expresses equality but *through* Him indicates subordination. They

[56] Mt. 5:11.

further insist that the Spirit must not be ranked with the Father or the Son, but under the Father and the Son, not in the same order of things as they are, but beneath them, not numbered with them. With technical jargon of this kind they pervert the uncluttered simplicity of the faith. They will not allow anyone else to remain ignorant of these matters, and so by their meddlesomeness have forfeited any plea that the ignorant might have.

14. First let us ask them this question: In what way do they say that the Son is after the Father? Is He later in time, or in rank, or in dignity? As far as time is concerned, no one is so senseless as to claim that the Maker of the ages holds a second place; no interval could possibly divide the natural union of Father and Son. Even limited human thought demonstrates that it is impossible for the Son to be younger that the Father; first, we cannot conceive of either apart from their relationship with each other, and second, the very idea of "coming later" is applied to something separated from the present by a smaller interval of time than something else which "came earlier." For instance, what happened in Noah's time precedes what happened to the men of Sodom because Noah is more remote from us that the men of Sodom, whose history seems closer to us because it is nearer to our own times. Now in addition to being impious, is it really not the height of folly to measure the life of Him who transcends all times and ages, whose existence is incalculably remote from the present? Things subject to birth and corruption are described as prior to one another; are we therefore to compare God the Father as superior to God the Son, who exists before the ages? The supreme eminence of the Father is inconceivable; thought and reflection are utterly unable to penetrate the begetting of the Lord. By means of two words St. John has admirably contained the concept within tangible bound-

aries: he says "In the *beginning was* the Word." [57]
Thought cannot reach beyond *was,* or the imagination
beginning. No matter how far your thoughts travel back-
ward, you cannot get beyond the *was.* No matter how hard
you strain to see what is beyond the Son, you will find
it impossible to pass outside the confines of the *beginning.*
Therefore, true religion teaches us to think of the Son
with the Father.

15. If they think that the Son sits below the Father,
in a lesser place, so that the Father sits above, and pushes
the Son to the next seat below, let them say so, and we
will be silent, since the absurdity of such a position will
be immediately made clear. Their thoughts are so incon-
sistent that they will not admit that the Father fills all
things. Anyone with a sound mind believes that God per-
vades everything, but these men divide up from down, not
remembering the psalmist's words: "If I ascend to heaven,
Thou art there! If I make my bed in Sheol, Thou art
there!" [58] Even if we ignore the stupidity of confining incorporeal beings in defined places, how can we possibly
excuse their shameless attack upon Scripture? Look at the
passages they contradict! "Sit at my right hand," [59] and
". . . He sat down at the right hand of the majesty of
God." [60] The expression "right hand" does not indicate
a lower place as they contend, but a relationship of equality. It cannot be understood as the physical right hand,
but rather the Scripture emphasizes the magnificence of
the Son's great dignity. It remains for our opponents to
explain how this phrase indicates inferior rank. Let them
learn that Christ is the power of God and the wisdom of
God,[61] and the image of the invisible God,[62] and the brightness of His glory,[63] and the one whom God the Father has

---

[57] Jn. 1:1.   [59] Ps. 110:1.   [61] I Cor. 1:24.   [63] Heb. 1:3.
[58] Ps. 139:8.   [60] Heb. 1:3.   [62] Col. 1:15.

sealed,[64] whom the Father has stamped with the image of His Person. Are we to call these and other passages like them in the Scriptures evidence that the Son holds a lower place, or are they public proclamations of the Only-Begotten's majesty and of His equal glory with the Father? Let them listen to the Lord Himself, who clearly declares that He shares equal glory and honor with the Father. He says, "He who has seen me has seen the Father" [65] and "when the Son comes in the glory of His Father" [66] and that "all may honor the Son, even as they honor the Father" [67] and "the only-begotten God who is in the bosom of the Father" [68] and "we have beheld His glory, glory as of the only-begotten of the Father." [69] They ignore these passages, and then assign to the Son the place reserved for His enemies. The Father's bosom is a worthy throne for His Son, but the footstool is reserved for those who have been forced to fall down before it.[70] We have only examined these passages briefly, in order to pass on to other questions. You may assemble these proofs at your leisure, and then you will see the exalted glory and preeminent power of the Only-Begotten. This evidence is not insignificant to the well-disposed listener, unless the terms "right hand" and "bosom" are interpreted in a fallen, fleshly sense, and used in an attempt to confine God within prescribed boundaries. Form, shape, and bodily position cannot be invented for God; these factors are alien to the absolute, the infinite, the incorporeal. What is worse, these ideas are derogatory to the Father when applied to the Son. They cannot reduce the Son's dignity, but those who repeat them incur the charge of blaspheming God, since any boldness directed to the Son is by logical necessity transferred to the Father. If someone assigns a higher place to the Father as His due, and says that the

---

[64] Jn. 6:27.   [66] Mk. 8:38.   [68] Jn. 1:18.   [70] Cf. Ps. 110:1.
[65] Jn. 14:9.   [67] Jn. 5:23.   [69] Jn. 1:14.

Only-Begotten Son sits below, he will discover himself to
have imagined God to possess physical properties. These
fantasies and delusions come from drunkenness and in-
sanity. The Lord taught men that "He who does not honor
the Son does not honor the Father;" [71] how then can anyone be part of true religion who refuses to worship and
glorify with the Father Him who is joined to the Father
in nature, glory, and dignity? What more can we say?
What just defense shall we have on the dread day of universal judgment? The Lord has clearly announced that
He will come in the glory of His Father.[72] Stephen saw
Jesus standing at the right hand of God;[73] Paul testified
in the Spirit concerning Christ, that He is at the right
hand of God; [74] the Father has said, "Sit at my right
hand," [75] and the Holy Spirit testifies that He sat down at
the right hand of the majesty of God.[76] He shares the
throne and the honor; shall we attempt to degrade Him
from His seat of equality to a lower place? Sitting, as opposed to standing, indicates that a nature is entirely fixed
and stable. When Baruch wishes to describe God's im-
mutability and immobility, he says, "Thou sittest forever
while we are forever passing away." [77] The place on the
right hand denotes equal dignity. How is it not reckless
to rob the Son of His position of equality in the doxology,
as if He deserved to be ranked in a lower place?

---

[71] Jn. 5:23.   [73] Acts 7:55.   [75] Ps. 110:1.   [77] Bar. 3:3.
[72] Mt. 16:27.   [74] Rom. 8:34.   [76] Heb. 8:1.

CHAPTER 7. *Against those who say that it is not suitable for "with whom" to be used in the Doxology concerning the Son, but that the proper phrase is "through whom."*

16. Our opponents say that the use of the phrase "with him" is completely alien and unknown, while "through him" occurs frequently in Scripture and is constantly used by the brethren. What can we say to this? Blessed are the ears that have not heard you, and the hearts that have been guarded against the poison of your words. But to you who love Christ I have this to say: the Church recognizes both usages, dismissing neither as excluding the other. Whenever we reflect on the majesty of the nature of the Only-Begotten, and the excellence of His dignity, we ascribe glory to Him *with* the Father. On the other hand, when we consider the abundant blessings He has given us, and how He has admitted us as co-heirs into God's household, we acknowledge that this grace works for us *through* Him and *in* Him. Therefore the best phrase when giving Him glory is *with whom* and the most appropriate for giving thanks is *through whom*. It is not true that the phrase *with whom* is alien to the usage of the faithful. Everyone who steadfastly values the old ways above these novelties, and who has preserved unchanged the tradition of the fathers both in the city and in the country, is familiar with this phrase. Rather, it is those never content with accepted ways who despise the old as being stale, constantly welcoming innovation, like worldlings who are always chasing after the latest fashion. Observe that country people cling to ancient patterns of speech, while the adroit language of these cunning disputants always bears the brand of the latest trends of thought. But as for us, what our fathers said, we repeat: the same glory is given to the Father and Son; therefore we offer the doxology to the Father *with* the Son. But we are not content simply because this is the tradition of the Fathers. What is important is that the Fathers followed the meaning of Scripture, beginning with the evidence which I have just extracted from the Scriptures and presented to you. The radiance is always considered with the glory that is its source, the image with its prototype, and always, the Son with the Father. One demands the existence of the other, and both are inseparably joined in name and in nature.

CHAPTER 8. *The many ways "through whom" is used, and the occasions when "with whom" is more suitable. Explanation of how the Son receives a commandment, and how He is sent.*

17. The apostle says, "I thank my God *through* Jesus Christ" [78] and *through* whom we have received grace and apostleship, to bring about the obedience of faith ... among all nations" [79] and "*through* Him we have obtained access to this grace in which we stand, and we rejoice." [80] He speaks here of the kindnesses which the Son has bestowed on us; sometimes He carries these good gifts of grace from the Father to us, and other times He leads us to the Father through Himself. When Paul says, "through whom we have received grace and apostleship" he indi-

---

[78] Rom. 1:8.   [79] Rom. 1:5.   [80] Rom. 5:2.

cates that these abundant blessings proceed from the Son,
and when he says "through Him we have obtained access"
he demonstrates that through Christ we have acquired
membership in God's household. Is it possible that our
acknowledgement of the blessings He has accomplished
for us reduces His glory? Is it not more true to say that
when we remember His mighty works, we find the proper
means of praise? This is why we find that the Scriptures
do not confine themselves to only one name when they
describe the Lord, nor are they limited to terms indicative
of His divine majesty. Sometimes words are used which
describe His nature, recognizing "the name which is above
every name," [81] the name of Jesus the *Son*. The Scriptures
say that He is truly the Son,[82] and Only-begotten God,[83]
Power of God,[84] Wisdom,[85] and Word.[86] Also, because of
the many ways grace is given to us poor men by Him
whose goodness and wisdom are manifold, He is described
by innumerable other titles: Shepherd, King, Physician,
Bridegroom, Way, Door, Fountain, Bread, Axe, and Rock.
These titles do not describe His nature, but, as I have
already said, are concerned with his manifold energies, by
which He satisfies the needs of each in His tenderhearted-
ness to His own creation. Those who flee to His ruling
care for refuge, and through patient endurance correct
their evil ways, He calls sheep, and He acknowledges Himself to be the *Shepherd* of those who hear His voice, refusing to listen to strange teachings. "My sheep hear my
voice," [87] He says. He is *King* of those who have risen to
a higher way of life, submitting themselves to their lawful
ruler. Because He leads men through the narrow gate of
His commandments to the practice of good deeds, and because He securely shuts in those who through faith in

---

[81] Phil. 2:9.   [84] I Cor. 1:24.   [86] Jn. 1:1.
[82] Mt. 14:33; 27:54.   [85] Idem.   [87] Jn. 10:27.
[83] Jn. 1:18.

Him find shelter in true wisdom, He is the *Door*. Therefore
He says, "If any one enters by Me, he ... will go in and
out and find pasture." [88] Because He is a mighty fortress
for the faithful, an unshaken and unbroken bullwark, He
is called *Rock*. It is with these titles, such as
Door or *Way*, that the phrase "through whom" is
most suitably used, but when He is glorified as God and
Son, it is *with* and together *with* the Father so that "at the
name of Jesus every knee should bow, in heaven and on
earth and under the earth, and every tongue confess that
Jesus Christ is Lord, to the glory of God the Father." [89]
Therefore we use both phrases, expressing His unique
dignity by one, and His grace to us by the other.

18.   Every kind of help comes to our souls *through*
Him, and an appropriate title has been devised for each
particular kind of care. When He presents a blameless soul
to Himself, a soul which like a pure virgin has neither
spot nor wrinkle, He is called *Bridegroom*, but when He
receives someone paralyzed by the devil's evil strokes, and
heals the heavy burden of his sins, He is called *Physician*.
Because He cares for us, will this make us think less of
Him? Or will we not be struck with amazement at our
Savior's mighty power and love for mankind, who patiently
endured to suffer our infirmities with us, and condescended
to our weakness? No heaven, or earth, or the great oceans,
or all creatures living in the waters and on dry land, or
plants, stars, air, and seasons, or the vast expanse of the
universe, can illustrate the surpassing greatness of God's
might so well as He has Himself. The infinite God, remaining changeless, assumed flesh and fought with death, free-
ing us from suffering by His own suffering! Even when
the Apostle says that "in all these things (tribulations and
sufferings) we are more than conquerors through Him who

---

[88] Jn. 10:9.   [89] Phil. 2:10-11.

loved us," [90] in a phrase of this kind there is no suggestion of any lowly and subordinate ministry, but rather it speaks of the good He has accomplished "in the strength of His might." [91] He Himself has bound the strong man and plundered His goods [92] — that is, us, who had been abased in every manner of evil — and made us into vessels fit for the Master's use, the use of our free will being made ready for any good work.[93] Thus through Him we have our approach to the Father, Who has transferred us from the dominion of darkness to share in the inheritance of the saints in light.[94] We must not think that the salvation the Son has won for us is the result of a slave's compulsory and subordinate service. No, He voluntarily accomplishes His plan out of goodness and compassion for His creation, fulfilling the Father's will. We follow true religion if we bear witness to the Son's power made manifest in everything He has fulfilled and accomplished, never separating His work from the Father's will. For instance, whenever the Lord is called the *Way*, we should be raised to a higher meaning, and not to the common understanding of the word. We understand the *Way* to be the road to perfection, advancing in order step by step through the words of righteousness and the illumination of knowledge, always yearning for that which lies ahead and straining toward the last mile, until we reach that blessed end, the knowledge of God, with which the Lord blesses those who believe in Him. For truly our Lord is a good Way, a straight road with no confusing forks or turns, leading us directly to the Father. "No one comes to the Father," He says, "except through Me." [95] Such is our way up to God through His Son.

19. Our next task is to discuss the treasury of bless-

---

[90] Rom. 8:37.   [92] Mt. 12:21.   [94] Cf. Col. 1:12-13.
[91] Eph. 6:10.   [93] Cf. II Tim. 2:21.   [95] Jn. 14:6.

ings which come from the Father through the Son to us.
All created nature, whether visible or spiritual, is held together by God's care: He who is the creating Word, the
only-begotten God. He bestows help on every creature
according to its need. He measures individual requirements,
and then distributes many different kinds of bounties. He
enlightens those who are confined in the darkness of ignorance; therefore He is called the True Light. He judges
every man according to the measure of his works, therefore He is called the righteous Judge. "The Father judges
no one, but has given all judgement to the Son." [96] He
raises up from the depths of sin those who have fallen from
resurrection. He accomplishes all things by His powerful
touch. He shepherds, He enlightens, He nourishes, He
leads, He heals, He raises up. He calls all things from non-
existence into being; once things are created He keeps
them in existence. Thus God's blessings reach us through
the Son, Who works in each case with greater speed than
words can describe. Neither lightning, or the speed of light
racing through the air, or a blink of the eyes, or the move-
ment of our thoughts, is as swift as the Son's working.
Divine energy surpasses everything in speed; it is faster
than birds, or the wind, or the revolution of the heavenly
bodies, or our very thoughts. It makes living creatures appear sluggish. What passage of time is needed by Him Who
"upholds the universe by His word of power?" [97] He does
not work by bodily strength, nor does He need the use
of hands in order to fashion things, but all created things
follow Him, offering Him their willing cooperation. As
Judith says, "The things Thou has foreordained present
themselves and say, 'We are here!' " [98] On the other hand,
we must not be so dazzled by the greatness of the Lord's
works that we imagine that He has no origin. What does
the self-existent One say about this? "I live through the

---

[96] Jn. 5:22.   [97] Heb. 1:3.   [98] Jud. 9:5-6.

Father," [99] and concerning divine power He says that "the
Son can do nothing of His own accord." [100] Where is the
source of His perfect wisdom? "The Father . . . has Himself given me commandment what to say and what to
speak."[101] Through all these words He guides us to the
knowledge of the Father; He directs our amazement at
everything He has made so that we may know the Father
through Him. The work of the Father is not separate or
distinct from the work of the Son; whatever the Son "sees
the Father doing . . . that the Son does likewise." [102] The
Father enjoys our awe at everything which proceeds from
the glory of the Only-begotten; He rejoices both in His
Son who accomplishes such deeds, and in the deeds themselves, and exults in being known as the Father of our
Lord Jesus Christ, "for whom and through whom all things
exist." [103] The Lord says, "All mine are thine," [104] as if
He were submitting His lordship over creation to the Father, but He also adds "thine are mine," [105] to show that
the creating command came from the Father to Him. The
Son did not need help to accomplish His work, nor are we
to believe that He received a separate commandment for
each portion of His work; such extreme inferiority would
be entirely inadequate to His divine glory. Rather, the
Word was full of His Father's grace; He shines forth from
the Father, and accomplishes everything according to His
Parent's plan. He is not different in essence, nor is He different in power from His Father, and if their power is
equal, then their works are the same. Christ is the power
of God, and the wisdom of God.[106] All things were made
through Him,[107] and all things were created through Him
and for Him,[108] not as if He were discharging the service

[99] Jn. 6:57.
[100] Jn. 5:19.
[101] Jn. 12:49.
[102] Jn. 5:19.
[103] Heb. 2:10.
[104] Jn. 17:10.
[105] Idem.
[106] I Cor. 1:24.
[107] Jn. 1:3.
[108] Col. 1:16.

of a slave, but instead He creatively fulfills the will of His Father.

20. When He says, "I have not spoken on my own authority," [109] and "As the Father has said unto me, so I speak," [110] and "the word which you hear is not mine but the Father's who sent me" [111] and "I do as the Father has commanded me," [112] He does not use language of this kind because He is incapable of His own choice, or is lawless, or has to wait for a prearranged signal. He wants to make it clear that His will is indissolubly united to the Father. We must not think that what He calls a "commandment" is an imperious order delivered by word of mouth by which the Father gives orders to His Son, as He would to a subordinate, telling Him what He should do. Instead, let us think in terms worthy of the Godhead, and realize that there is a transmission of will, like the reflection of an object in a mirror, which reaches from Father to Son without passage of time. "The Father loves the Son, and shows Him all that He Himself is doing." [113] Everything the Father has also belongs to the Son; He does not acquire it little by little, but has it all at once. In the world of men, when a workmen has been taught his craft, and had solid experience as well as a long period of training, he is able to begin work for himself, using the techniques he has learned. Does the wisdom of God, who fashioned all creation, who is eternally perfect, wise without being taught, or the power of God, in whom are hid all the treasures of wisdom and knowledge,[114] need to be given piecemeal instructions in order to determine the type and the extent of His operations? I presume by the vanity of your ideas that you intend to open a school, in which you will have the Father take His seat in the teacher's place,

---

[109] Jn. 12:49.   [111] Jn. 14:24.   [113] Jn. 5:20.
[110] Jn. 12:50.   [112] Jn. 14:31.   [114] Col. 2:3.

and the Son stand in front of Him like an ignorant school-boy, advancing in wisdom and perfection with the assistance of lessons given to Him bit by bit. If you consistently follow this train of thought, you will turn the Son into the eternal student, who is never able to reach the end of His studies, since the Father's wisdom is infinite, and the end of the infinite can never be reached. Anyone who will not admit that the Son has all things from the beginning must also admit that He will never reach perfection. I am ashamed at how low my thoughts have been dragged by following this notion to its end. Let us return to the higher aspects of our discussion.

21. "He who has seen me has seen the Father;" [115] this does not mean that he has seen the image and the form of the divine nature, since the divine nature is simple, not composed of various parts. Goodness of will is a current in the stream of the divine essence, and thus is perceived to be the same in the Father and the Son. What then is meant by "He humbled Himself and became obedient unto death" [116] or "God . . . did not spare His own Son but gave Him up for us all?" [117] It means that what the Son does for men He accomplishes by means of the Sonship He receives from the Father. Listen to these words also: "Christ redeemed us from the curse of the law" [118] and "while we were yet sinners Christ died for us." [119] Pay close attention to the Lord's words; (whenever He instructs us about the Father),[120] He knows that by using terms of personal authority, such as "I will; be clean," [121]

---

[115] Jn. 14:9.   [117] Rom. 8:32.   [119] Rom. 5:8.

[116] Phil 2:8.   [118] Gal. 3:13.

[120] This phrase is most obscure, and I have not found a suitable explanation for it in any commentator. I have enclosed it in parentheses because it seems to have nothing to do with what precedes or follows.

[121] Mt. 8:3.

and "Peace! Be still!" [122] and "But I say to you . . ." [123]
and "You deaf and dumb spirit, I command you," [124] and
other similar expressions, we will be led to recognize Him
as our Master and Creator. This recognition will teach
us to know the *Father* of our Master and Creator, and
the true doctrine will be upheld on all sides: the Father
creates through the Son. This does not insinuate that the
Father's creation is imperfect, or that the Son's energy
is feeble, but shows their unity of will. Therefore the expression *through whom* admits of a principal Cause, but
cannot be used an an objection against the efficient Cause.

CHAPTER 9. *Distinctive ideas concerning
                 the Spirit which follow the teachings
                 of Scripture.*

22.   We shall now examine what kinds of ideas about
the Spirit we hold in common, as well as those which we
have gathered from the Scriptures, or received from the
unwritten tradition of the Fathers. First of all, who can
listen to the Spirit's titles and not be lifted up in his soul?
Whose thoughts would not be raised to contemplate the
supreme nature? He is called the Spirit of God, the Spirit
of truth who proceeds from the Father,[125] right Spirit, willing Spirit. His first and most proper title is Holy Spirit,
a name most especially appropriate to everything which
is incorporeal, purely immaterial, and indivisible. That is
why the Lord taught the Samaritan woman, who thought
that God had to be worshipped in specific places, that
"God is Spirit." [126] He wanted to show that an incorporeal
being cannot be circumscribed. When we hear the word
"spirit" it is impossible for us to conceive of something

---

[122] Mk. 4:39.   [123] Mt. 5:22 ff.   [124] Mk. 9:25.   [125] Jn. 15:26.

whose nature can be circumscribed or is subject to change or variation, or is like a creature in any way. Instead, we are compelled to direct our thoughts on high, and to think of an intelligent being, boundless in power, of unlimited greatness, generous in goodness, whom time cannot measure. All things thirsting for holiness turn to Him; [127] everything living in virtue never turns away from Him. He waters them with His life-giving breath and helps them reach their proper fulfillment. He perfects all other things, and Himself lacks nothing; He gives life to all things, and is never depleted. He does not increase by additions, but is always complete, self-established, and present everywhere. He is the source of sanctification, spiritual light, who gives illumination to everyone using His powers to search for the truth — and the illumination He gives is Himself. His nature is unapproachable; only through His goodness are we able to draw near it. He fills all things with His power, but only those who are worthy may share it. He distributes His energy in proportion to the faith of the recipient, not confining it to a single share. He is simple in being; His powers are manifold: they are wholly present everywhere and in everything. He is distributed but does not change. He is shared, yet remains whole. Consider the analogy of the sunbeam: each person upon whom its kindly light falls rejoices as if the sun existed for him alone, yet it illumines land and sea, and is master of the atmosphere. In the same way, the Spirit is given to each one who receives Him as if He were the possession of that person alone, yet He sends forth sufficient grace to fill all the

---

[126] Jn. 4:24.

[127] It must be borne in mind that "τὸ πνεῦμα" is a neuter form, and perhaps the pronoun "it" would be more appropriate. Nevertheless, the use of the neuter gender in English would depersonalize the Holy Spirit; therefore I have chosen the masculine, somewhat arbitrarily. Both the neuter and the masculine may be found in Scripture.

universe. Everything that partakes of His grace is filled with joy according to its capacity — the capacity of its nature, not of His power.

23. The Spirit does not take up His abode in someone's life through a physical approach; how could a corporeal being approach the Bodiless one? Instead, the Spirit comes to us when we withdraw ourselves from evil passions, which have crept into the soul through its friendship with the flesh, alienating us from a close relationship with God. Only when a man has been cleansed from the shame of his evil, and has returned to his natural beauty, and the original form of the Royal Image has been restored in him, is it possible for him to approach the Paraclete. Then, like the sun, He will show you in Himself the image of the invisible, and with purified eyes you will see in this blessed image the unspeakable beauty of its prototype. Through Him hearts are lifted up, the infirm are held by the hand, and those who progress are brought to perfection. He shines upon those who are cleansed from every spot, and makes then spiritual men through fellowship with Himself. When a sunbeam falls on a transparent substance, the substance itself becomes brilliant, and radiates light from itself. So too Spirit-bearing souls, illumined by Him, finally become spiritual themselves, and their grace is sent forth to others. From this comes knowledge of the future, understanding of mysteries, apprehension of hidden things, distribution of wonderful gifts, heavenly citizenship, a place in the choir of angels, endless joy in the presence of God, becoming like God, and, the highest of all desires, becoming God. These are only a few of the many things we have been taught concerning the greatness, dignity, and working of the Holy Spirit, and we have learned them from the Spirit's own words. But now we must attempt to refute our opponents' false ideas which have been directed against us.

CHAPTER 10. *Against those who say that it is not right to rank the Holy Spirit with the Father and the Son.*

24. They say that it is not suitable to rank the Holy Spirit with the Father and the Son, because He is different in nature and inferior in dignity from them. But it is fitting for us to respond to them with the apostles' words: "We must obey God rather than men." [128] When the Lord established the baptism of salvation, did He not clearly command His disciples to baptize all nations "in the name of the Father, and of the Son, and of the Holy Spirit"? [129] He did not disdain His fellowship with the Holy Spirit, but these men say that we should not rank Him with the Father and the Son. Are they not openly disregarding God's commandment? If they will not admit that this arrangement of Father, Son, and Spirit testifies to their union and fellowship, let them explain to us why we should agree with their opinion. How could Father, Son, and Spirit be united in a different or more suitable way? If indeed the Lord did *not* speak of Himself, the Father, and the Spirit as being united in baptism, then let our opponents blame us for having invented this doctrine. But no one is so shameless that he will deny the obvious meaning of the words which clearly say the Spirit *is* one with the Father and the Son. So let our opponents be silent; as for us, we will follow the words of Scripture.

25. All the weapons of war have been prepared against us; every intellectual missile is aimed at us; the blasphemers' tongues strike us harder than the stones thrown at Stephen by the Christ-killers of old. They pre-

---

[128] Acts 5:29.   [129] Matt. 28:19.

tend that their attack is directed against us, but they cannot conceal that their real purpose is much worse. They say that they have prepared this siege and these snares against us; they have taken inventory of each man's strength and cunning and advance against us with shouts. But the object of their attack is the faith itself. The one aim of the whole band of these enemies of sound doctrine is to shake the faith of Christ down to its foundations, by utterly levelling apostolic tradition to the ground. They clamor for written proofs and reject the unwritten testimony of the Fathers as worthless, proving themselves worse than debtors who refuse to pay what they owe when there is no written evidence of the loan. But we will never surrender the truth; we will not betray the defense like cowards. The Lord has delivered to us a necessary and saving dogma: the Holy Spirit is to be ranked with the Father. Our opponents do not agree; instead they divide and tear away the Spirit from the Father, transforming His nature to that of a ministering spirit. Can anyone dispute that they make their own blasphemy more authoritative than the law of the Lord? But let us abandon these rivalries for now, and examine the following questions.

26. What makes us Christians? "Our faith," everyone would answer. How are we saved? Obviously through the regenerating grace of baptism. How else could we be? We are confirmed in our understanding that salvation comes through Father, Son, and Holy Spirit. Shall we cast away the standard of teaching we received? This would surely be grounds for great sorrow; if we now reject what we accepted at baptism, we will be found to be further away from our salvation than when we first believed. We would be no different from someone who died without baptism, or who had been baptized with an unacceptable form. We made this profession when we first entered the Church; we were delivered from idols and came before the living

God. Whoever does not hold fast to this confession as his sure foundation at all times, to the end of his life, makes himself a stranger to God's promises. That man's profession of faith is recorded in his own handwriting and it will testify against him. If baptism is the beginning of my life, and the day of my regeneration is the first of days, it is obvious that the words spoken when I received the grace of adoption are more honorable than any spoken since. How could I be snared by these subtle arguments, and abandon the tradition which led me to the light, and gave me the blessing of divine knowledge? Through this confession I was made a child of God, I, who was His enemy for so long because of my sins. May I pass from this life to the Lord with this confession on my lips. I exhort them to keep the faith inviolate until the day of Christ's coming: they must not divide the Spirit from the Father and the Son, but must preserve in the profession of faith and in the doxology the teaching they received at their baptism.

CHAPTER 11. *Those who deny the Spirit are transgressors.*

27. Who has woe? Who are afflicted? Who are headed for agony, darkness, eternal damnation? The transgressors; those who deny the faith. What is the proof of their denial? They have abandoned what they professed when they entered God's household. What did they profess? Faith in the Father, the Son, and the Holy Spirit. They uttered these saving words when they renounced the devil and his angels. How can the children of light describe such men? They are transgressors, since they have broken the saving covenant. What else can denying God, denying Christ, be called, but transgressing? How do you wish me to label those who deny the Spirit? They must be described in the same way, for they have broken their covenant with God. Professing faith in Him wins the blessings of true religion, but damnation will be the wages of the godless who have denied Him. To forsake the profession of faith is a fearful thing, and they have abandoned it not through fear of fire, or sword, or cross, or flogging, or the wheel, or the rack, but only because they have been led astray by the deceitful sophistries of the Spirit-deniers (pneumato-machoi). I swear to every man who confesses Christ but denies the Father: Christ will profit him nothing. If a man calls upon God, but rejects the Son, his faith is empty. If someone rejects the Spirit, his faith in the Father and the Son is made useless; it is impossible to believe in the Father and the Son without the presence of the Spirit. He who rejects the Spirit rejects the Son, and he who rejects the Son rejects the Father. "No one can say 'Jesus is Lord' except in the Holy Spirit," [130] and "no one has ever seen God; the only-begotten God, who is in the bosom of the Father, He has make Him known." [131] Such a person has no part in true worship. It is impossible to worship the Son except in the Holy Spirit; it is impossible to call upon the Father except in the Spirit of adoption.

CHAPTER 12. *Against those who maintain that baptism in the Lord's name alone is sufficient.*

28. Do not be misled because the Apostle frequently omits the names of the Father and the Holy Spirit when he speaks of baptism. Do not imagine because of this that

---

[130] I Cor. 12:3.   [131] Jn. 1:18.

the invocation of their names has been omitted. St. Paul
says, "As many of you as were baptized into Christ have
put on Christ" [132] and ". . . all of us who have been baptized into Christ Jesus were baptized into His death." [133]
To address Christ in this way is a complete profession of
faith, because it clearly reveals that God anoints the Son
(the Anointed One) with the unction of the Spirit. We
can learn this from Peter's words in Acts: "God anointed
Jesus of Nazareth with the Holy Spirit," [134] or from Isaiah:
"The Spirit of the Lord God is upon me, because the
Lord has anointed me." [135] or from the Psalms: "Therefore God, your God, has anointed you with the oil of
gladness above your fellows." [136] But Scripture also clearly
speaks of baptism in the context of the Spirit alone, e.g.,
"For by one Spirit we are all baptized into one body." [137]
There are other passages which agree with this: "You
shall be baptized with the Holy Spirit," [138] and "He will
baptize you with the Holy Spirit." [139] No one would claim
that on the basis of these passages the invocation of the
Spirit's name alone makes baptism complete and perfect;
the tradition we have received through life-giving grace
must remain unchanged forever. He who redeemed our
life from corruption gave us the power to be renewed, and
the source of this power is hidden in an indescribable
mystery. It brings great salvation to our souls, but to add
or to take anything away from it is to forfeit eternal life.
The position of the baptizer who separates the Spirit from
the Father and the Son is precarious indeed, since the baptism received from him is useless. How can we be safe
if we tear the Spirit away from the Father and the Son?
Faith and baptism are two inseparably united means of
salvation. Faith is perfected through baptism; the founda-

---

[132] Gal. 3:27.   [135] Is. 61:1.   [138] Acts 1:5.
[133] Rom. 6:3.   [136] Ps. 45:7.   [139] Lk. 3:16.
[134] Acts 10:38.   [137] I Cor. 12:13.

tion of baptism is faith, and both are fulfilled through the same names. First we believe in the Father, Son, and Holy Spirit; then we are baptized in the name of the Father, the Son, and the Holy Spirit. The profession of faith leads us to salvation, and then baptism follows, sealing our affirmation.

CHAPTER 13. *Why St. Paul associates the angels with the Father and the Son.*

29. Someone might object that beings occasionally listed with the Father and the Son are not always glorified together with them. For example, St. Paul associates the angels with them in his charge to Timothy: "In the presence of God and of Christ Jesus and of the elect angels I charge you . . ." [140] We do not separate the angels from the rest of creation, nor would we permit them to be numbered with the Father and the Son, so why should we understand the Spirit any differently? This argument is so ridiculous it does not even deserve a reply, but I answer as follows: Perhaps one's fellow-slave (i.e. an angel) could testify to a mild and gentle judge — especially to Him who is so fair to those arraigned before Him, showing them that His decisions are undeniably righteous. But if a slave is to be made free, and called a son of God, and brought from death into life, it can only be accomplished by Him who shares our nature and delivers it from slavery. How could we be joined to God's household by someone who does not share our nature? How could we be freed by someone who bears the yoke of a servant? One does not speak of the Spirit and of angels as if they were equals;

---

[140] I Tim. 5:21.

the Spirit is the Lord of life and the angels are our helpers, our fellow-servants, faithful witnesses of the truth. It is customary for the saints to deliver God's commandments in the presence of witnesses. St. Paul says to Timothy: ". . . what you have heard from me before many witnesses entrust to faithful men." [141] He asks the angels to testify with him, because he knows that angels will be present when the Lord comes in the glory of His Father to judge the world in righteousness. The Lord says, "Everyone who acknowledges me before men, the Son of man also will acknowledge before the angels of God, but he who denies me before men, will be denied before the angels of God." [142] Paul says in another place, "when the Lord Jesus is revealed from heaven with his mighty angels." [143] He testifies before the angels now, so that they will testify for him on the great day of judgement.

30. Paul is not alone in this; generally all those who have been entrusted with the ministry of the word never cease asking for witnesses. They call upon heaven and earth to testify on their behalf, since every deed is accomplished in the presence of the earth and the skies, and they will also be present on that day when every man will be judged according to his works. For this reason Scripture says, "He calls to the heavens above, and to the earth, that he may judge his people." [144] After Moses had proclaimed the law to the people, he said, "I call heaven and earth to witness against you this day," [145] and he begins his song as follows: "Give ear O heavens, and I will speak; and let the earth hear the words of my mouth." [146] Isaiah says: "Hear, O heaven, and give ear, O earth," [147] and Jeremiah describes how the heavens were horrified

---

[141] II Tim. 2:2.
[142] Lk. 12:8-9.
[143] II Thess. 1:7.
[144] Ps. 50:4.
[145] Deut. 4:26.
[146] Deut. 32:1.
[147] Is. 1:2.

when they heard the description of the people's unholy deeds. "Be appalled, O heavens, at this; be shocked, be utterly desolate, says the Lord, for my people have committed two evils." [148] Paul calls the angels to testify because he knows they have been set in command over men as teachers and guardians. Joshua, the son of Nun, even calls a stone to give testimony (a heap of stones had already been called to testify between Jacob and Laban) [149] when he said: "Behold, this stone shall be a witness against us; for it has heard all the works of the Lord which He spoke to us; therefore it shall be a witness against you, lest you deal falsely with your God." [150] Perhaps he believed that the power of God would enable the stones to cry out in testimony against the transgressors or at least that every man's conscience would be wounded by the force of the reminder. So those who have been entrusted with the care of souls provide various kinds of witnesses to testify at a future date. But the Spirit is organically united with God, not because of the needs of each moment, but through communion in the divine nature. He is joined to the Lord; He is not brought in by our efforts.

CHAPTER 14. *An answer to the objection that some were baptized into Moses, and believed in him. Also, some remarks concerning typology.*

31. Some say that just because we are baptized in the Spirit, it is not sufficient reason for the Spirit to be ranked with God. In the Old Testament, "all were baptized into Moses in the cloud and in the sea." [151] Furthermore, it is nothing new to profess faith in men: "they

---

[148] Jer. 2:12-13.   [149] Cf. Gen. 31:46ff.   [150] Jos. 24:27.   [151] I Cor. 10:2.

believed in the Lord *and* in his servant Moses." [152] Therefore, they ask, why do we exalt and magnify the Holy
Spirit as if He were above creation, on the grounds of faith
and baptism? There is evidence that the same faith has
been professed in men in days gone by. How can we
answer this? We believe in the Spirit as we believe in the
Father and the Son, and we are baptized in the name of
each. What is said concerning Moses and the cloud is a
shadow or type. Surely you realize that just because divine
things are foreshadowed by finite, human things, we cannot conclude that the divine nature is finite. Divine things
are very often prefigured by means of shadowy types. Typology points out what is to be expected, indicating through
imitation what is to happen before it happens. Adam was
a type of Him who was to come; [153] "the Rock was
Christ" [154] typologically, and the water from the rock was
a type of the living power of the Word, for He says, "If
anyone thirst, let him come to Me and drink." [155] The
manna was a type of the living bread which came down
from heaven,[156] and the serpent suspended on the pole [157]
was a type of the saving passion accomplished on the
cross, since the life of every one who looked at the serpent
was preserved. Similarly, the history of Israel's exodus
was recorded to typify those who would be saved through
baptism. The firstborn of the Israelites were saved in the
same way as the bodies of the baptized: through grace
given to those who were marked with blood. The blood
of the lamb is a type of the blood of Christ, and the firstborn is a type of the first-formed man. Since the first-
formed man necessarily exists in each of us and will continue to be transmitted among us until the end, it is said
that in Adam we all die,[158] and that death reigned until

---

[152] Ex. 14:31.   [155] Jn. 7:37.   [157] Num. 21:8ff.
[153] Rom. 5:14.   [156] Jn. 6:41.   [158] I Cor. 15:22.
[154] I Cor. 10:4.

the fulfillment of the law and the coming of Christ. The firstborn were preserved by God from the destroyer's touch to show that we who are made alive in Christ no longer die in Adam. At the time of the exodus, the sea and the cloud led the people from amazement to faith, but they also typified the grace which was yet to come. "Whoever is wise, let him understand these things" [159]: how the baptism in the sea which brought about Pharaoh's demise typifies the washing which makes the devil's tyranny depart. The sea killed the enemy in its waves, and baptism kills the enmity between us and God. The people emerged from the sea unharmed, and we come up from the water as alive from the dead, saved by the grace of Him Who has called us. The cloud is a shadow of the Spirit's gifts, for He cools the flames of our passions through the mortification of our bodies.

32.   What can be said? Is the grace of baptism lessened because it was already foreshadowed by Israel's baptism into Moses? If this is true, and if we prejudice the dignity of any one of our privileges by comparing it to its type, we would find that not a single one is anything especially great. God's love for man, though He gave His Only-Begotten Son for our sins, would be nothing great or extraordinary; after all, Abraham did not spare his only son. What would be so glorious about the Lord's passion? A ram was a suitable substitution for Isaac, who prefigured the sacrifice. What would be so awesome about the descent into hell? Had not Jonah already typified His three days and three nights of death? The same comparison is made in the case of baptism by those who judge the reality by the shadow. They compare what was typified to the type, and by using Moses and the sea they attempt to undermine the entire dispensation of the Gospel. What

---

[159] Hos. 14:9.

remission of sins or renewal of life was found in the Red
Sea? What spiritual gift comes through Moses? Is deadness
to sin found there? Those men did not die with Christ;
therefore they were not raised with Him. They did not
bear the image of the heavenly man;[160] they did not
carry the dying of Jesus in their bodies;[161] they did not
put off the old man or put on the new man, who is being
renewed after the image of his Creator.[162] Why do you
compare these baptisms? The only thing they have in common is the fact that they are baptisms; the difference between them is as great as the difference between dream
and reality, or between shadows and substantial figures.

33. If we adopt our opponents' position, not only will
faith in Moses reveal that faith in the Spirit is worth little,
but it will also diminish our confession of faith in the God
of the universe. It is written that the people believed in
the Lord and in His servant Moses.[163] Notice that Moses
is mentioned together with God, not with the Spirit; he
was a type of Christ, not of the Spirit. Under the ministry
of the law, he himself foreshadowed the Mediator between
God and men, Christ Jesus;[164] he did not prefigure the
Spirit when he mediated between God and the people. The
law was ordained by angels through an intermediary,[165]
namely Moses, because of the people's proposal: "You
speak to us, and we will hear; but let not God speak to us,
lest we die." [166] Faith in Moses was supposed to lead to
faith in the Lord, the Mediator between God and men,
Who said: "If you believed Moses, you would believe
Me." [167] Is our faith in the Lord a trifle, because it was
foreshadowed by Moses? Even if men were baptized into
Moses, it does not mean that the grace given by the Spirit

---

[160] I Cor. 15:49.   [163] Ex. 14:31.   [166] Ex. 20:19.
[161] II Cor. 4:10.   [164] I Tim. 2:5.   [167] Jn. 5:46.
[162] Col. 3:9-10.   [165] Gal. 3:19.

is small. Furthermore, it is customary for the Scripture to personify the law in Moses, as in the passage, "They have Moses (i.e., the law) and the prophets." [168] Therefore when it says that they were baptized into Moses, it means that they were baptized into the law. Why do these enemies of the truth attempt through shadows and types to show contempt to the "pride of our hope," [169] the rich gift of our God and Savior who through regeneration renews our youth like the eagle's? Surely only an infantile mind, like a baby who can only drink milk, is ignorant of the great mystery of our salvation. Education progressed gradually; the school of righteousness attempts to bring us to perfection by first teaching us easy, elementary lessons suited for our limited intelligence. Then God, Who provides us with every good thing, leads us to the truth, by gradually accustoming our darkened eyes to its great light. In the deep riches of His wisdom and the unsearchable judgements of His intelligence, He spares our weakness, and prescribes a gentle treatment. He knows our eyes are accustomed to dim shadows, so He uses these at first. Then He shows us the sun's reflection in water, so as to spare us from being blinded by its pure light. The law was a shadow of things to come, and the teachings of the prophets were a reflection of truth. He devised them to train the eyes of our hearts, so that we could make an easy transition to the secret and hidden wisdom of God, which God decreed before the ages for our glorification. [170] We have spoken sufficiently concerning typology; it is not possible to linger on this topic any longer. If we did, tangential discussions would become many times bulkier than our main argument!

---

[168] Lk. 16:29.   [169] Heb. 3:6.   [170] I Cor. 2:7.

CHAPTER 15. *Reply to the objection that
we are baptized into water.
Concerning baptism in general.*

34. The arguments of our opponents know no bounds.
How can I answer this one? We are baptised into water,
they say, and surely we will not honor water more than
the rest of creation, or give water a share of the honor due
the Father and the Son. As might be expected, these men
argue like raging warriors sparing no attempt in their attack when they are offended. They have allowed their
passions to obscure their reasoning. But we will not reject
a discussion even of these questions. How can we teach
the ignorant, if we retreat from evildoers? Let us regress
for a moment, and prepare our strategy.

35. God our Savior planned to recall man from the
fall. Man's disobedience separated him from God's household, and God wished to bring him back. This is why
Christ took flesh, and accomplished everything described
in the Gospels: His sufferings, the cross, the tomb, the
resurrection, so that man might be saved through imitation
of Christ and receive his original birthright. If we are to
be perfect we must not only imitate Christ's meekness,
humility, and longsuffering, but His death as well. Paul
surely was an imitator of Christ, and he says, "that I may
know Him and the power of His resurrection, and may
share His sufferings, becoming like Him in His death, that
if possible I may attain the resurrection from the dead." [171]
How can we become like Him in His death? [172] By being
buried with Him in baptism. [173] What kind of burial is it,
and what is gained from such imitation? First, it is necessary

[171] Phil. 3:10-11.   [172] Rom. 6:5.   [173] Rom. 6:4.

that the old way of life be terminated, and this is impossible unless a man is born again, as the Lord has said.[174] Regeneration, as its very name reveals, is a beginning of a second life. Before beginning a second life, one must put an end to the first. When a runner has to run around the post at the end of the racetrack in order to return on the other side of the course, he has to stop and pause momentarily, in order to negotiate such a sharp turn. So also if we are going to change our lives, death must come between what has already happened (ending it) and what is just beginning. How can we accomplish this descent into death? By imitating the burial of Christ through baptism. The bodies of those being baptized are buried in the water. Thus baptism signifies the putting off of the works of the flesh, as the Apostle says: "In Him also you were circumcised with a circumcision made without hands, by putting off the body of flesh in the circumcision of Christ; and you were buried with Him in baptism." [175] The filth which has grown on the soul by the working of a carnal mind is washed away. "Wash me, and I shall be whiter than snow." [176] In this respect we differ from the Jews: they wash themselves after each defilement, but we know that the baptism of salvation is received only once, since He died for the world once, and rose from the dead once, and baptism is a figure of His death and resurrection. The Lord who gives us life also gave us the baptismal covenant, which contains an image of both death and life. The image of death is fulfilled in the water, and the Spirit gives us the pledge of life. Therefore it is clear why water is associated with the Spirit: because of baptism's dual purpose. On the one hand, the body of sin is destroyed, that it may never bear fruit for death. On the other hand, we are made to live by the Spirit, and bear fruit in holiness. The water receives our body as a tomb, and so becomes the image of death, while

---

[174] Jn. 3:3.   [175] Col. 2:11-12.   [176] Ps. 51:7.

the Spirit pours in life-giving power, renewing in souls which were dead in sin the life they first possessed. This is what it means to be born again of water and Spirit: the water accomplishes our death, while the Spirit raises us to life. This great sign of baptism is fulfilled in three immersions, with three invocations, so that the image of death might be completely formed, and the newly-baptized might have their souls enlightened with divine knowledge. If there is any grace in the water, it does not come from the nature of the water, but from the Spirit's presence, since baptism is not a removal of dirt from the body, but an appeal to God for a clear conscience.[177] The Lord describes in the Gospel the pattern of life we must be trained to follow after the (baptismal) resurrection: gentleness, endurance, freedom for the defiling love of pleasure, and from covetousness. We must be determined to acquire in this life all the qualities of the life to come. To define the Gospel as a description of what resurrectional life should be like seems to be correct and appropriate, as far as I am concerned. Now let us return to our argument.

36. Through the Holy Spirit comes our restoration to Paradise, our ascension to the Kingdom of heaven, our adoption as God's sons, our freedom to call God our Father, our becoming partakers of the grace of Christ, being called children of light, sharing in eternal glory, and in a word, our inheritance of the fullness of blessing, both in this world and the world to come. Even while we wait for the full enjoyment of the good things in store for us, by the Holy Spirit we are able to rejoice through faith in the promise of the graces to come. If the promise itself is so glorious, what must its fulfillment be like? We are also able to distinguish between the grace that comes from the Spirit and mere baptism in water. John baptized in

---

[177] I Pet. 3:21.

water for repentance, but our Lord Jesus Christ baptized in the Holy Spirit. John said, "I baptize you with water, for repentance, but He who is coming after me is mightier than I, whose sandals I am not worthy to carry; He will baptize you with the Holy Spirit and with fire." [178] He calls our examination at the judgment a baptism by fire, as when the Apostle says "each men's work will become manifest, for the Day will disclose it, because it will be revealed with fire and the fire will test what sort of work each one has done." [179] Before our day there were some who fought for the true faith, and died for Christ's sake, not only symbollically, but in actual fact. They had no need of the outward sign of water to be saved, since they were baptized in their own blood. I mention this not because I wish to belittle baptism by water, but to overthrow the arguments of those who pit themselves against the Spirit, confusing things which are distinct, and comparing things that admit of no comparison.

CHAPTER 16. *The Holy Spirit cannot be separated from the Father and the Son in any way, whether it be in the creation of perceptible objects, the ordering of human affairs, or the coming judgment.*

37. Let us return to the point we first raised: that in everything the Holy Spirit is indivisibly and inseparably joined to the Father and the Son. St. Paul writes as follows to the Corinthians concerning the gift of tongues: "But if all prophesy, and an unbeliever or outsider enters, he is

---

[178] Mt. 3:11.   [179] I Cor. 3:13.

convicted by all, he is called to account by all, the secrets of his heart are disclosed; and so, falling on his face, he will worship God and declare that God is really among you." [180] If God is recognized to be present among prophets because their prophesying is a gift of the Spirit, let our opponents determine what place they will give to the Holy Spirit. Will they rank Him with God, or will they push Him down to a creature's place? Peter said to Sapphira, "How is it that you have agreed together to tempt the Spirit of the Lord? You have not lied to men but to God," [181] and this shows that to sin against the Holy Spirit is to sin against God. Understand from this that in every operation, the Holy Spirit is indivisibly united with the Father and the Son. God works in various ways, and the Lord serves in various capacities, but the Holy Spirit is also present of His own will, dispensing gifts to everyone according to each man's worth. Scripture says, "Now there are varieties of gifts, but the same Spirit; and there are varieties of service, but the same Lord; and there are varieties of working, but it is the same God who inspires them all in every one." [182] It also says, "All these are inspired by one and the same Spirit, who apportions to each one individually as He wills." [183] Just because the Apostle in the above passage mentions the Spirit first, and the Son second, and God the Father third, do not assume that he has reversed their rank. Notice that he is speaking the same way we do when we receive gifts: first we thank the messenger who brought the gift; next we remember him who sent it, and finally we raise our thoughts to the fountain and source of all gifts.

38. The communion of the Spirit with the Father and the Son may be understood by considering the creation of

---

[180] I Cor. 14:24-25.
[181] Acts 5:9,4.
[182] I Cor. 12:4-6.
[183] I Cor. 12:11.

the angels. The pure, spiritual, and transcendent powers
are called holy, because they have received holiness from
the grace of the Holy Spirit. The historian has described
for us only the creation of visible things and passes over
the creation of the bodiless hosts in silence. But from
visible things we are able to construct analogies of invisible
things, and so we glorify the Maker in whom all things
were created, in heaven and on earth, visible and invisible,
whether thrones or dominions or principalities or author-
ities,[184] or any other reason-endowed nature whose name
we do not know. When you consider creation I advise you
to first think of Him who is the first cause of everything
that exists: namely, the Father, and then of the Son, who
is the creator, and then the Holy Spirit, the perfector. So
the ministering spirits exist by the will of the Father, are
brought into being by the work of the Son, and are perfected by the presence of the Spirit, since angels are perfected by perseverance in holiness. And let no one accuse
me of saying that there are three unoriginate persons, or
that the work of the Son is imperfect. The Originator of
all things is One: He creates through the Son and perfects
through the Spirit. The Father's work is in no way imperfect, since He accomplishes all in all, nor is the Son's work
deficient if it is not completed by the Spirit. The Father
creates through His will alone and does not *need* the Son,
yet chooses to work through the Son. Likewise the Son
works as the Father's likeness, and needs no other cooperation, but He chooses to have His work completed
through the Spirit. "By the Word of the Lord the heavens
were made, and all their host by the Spirit of His mouth." [185]
The Word is not merely air set in motion by the organs
of speech, nor is the Spirit of His mouth an exhalation of
the lungs, but the Word is He who was with God in the
beginning, and was God [186] and the Spirit of God's mouth

---

[184] Col. 1:16.   [185] Ps. 32:6, (LXX).   [186] Jn. 1:21.

ON THE HOLY SPIRIT

is the Spirit of truth who proceeds from the Father.[187]
Perceive these three: the Lord who commands, the Word
who creates, and the Spirit who strengthens. What kind
of strengthening is it? Perfection in holiness, which expresses itself in an unyielding, unchangeable commitment
to goodness. Such holiness is impossible without the Spirit.
The angelic powers are not by their own nature holy;
otherwise there would be no difference between them and
the Holy Spirit. Rather, they are sanctified by the Holy
Spirit in proportion to their excellence. When we consider
a branding-iron we also immediately remember that fire
is required to heat it, yet we would not claim that the
iron and the fire are the same substance. The angels are
a similar case; they are essentially aerial spirits, composed
of immaterial fire, as it is written, "He makes His angels
spirits, and His ministers a flaming fire." [188] They exist in
space, and when they are seen by those who are worthy,
they assume an appropriate physical form. Holiness is not
part of their essence; it is accomplished in them through
communion with the Spirit. They keep their rank by perse-
vering in goodness, by freely choosing to never abandon
serving Him, who is good by nature. If we agree that the
Spirit is subordinate, then the choirs of angels are destroyed, the ranks of archangels are abolished, and everything is thrown into confusion, since their life loses all
law, order, or boundary. How can the angels cry "Glory
to God in the highest," [189] unless the Spirit enables them
to do so? "No one speaking by the Spirit of God
ever says, 'Jesus be cursed!' and no one can say 'Jesus
is Lord' except by the Holy Spirit." [190] Evil and hostile
spirits might say such a thing as 'Jesus be cursed,' and the
existence of fallen spirits proves our statement that the
angels have free will. They are free to choose either good

---

[187] Jn. 15:26.   [189] Lk. 2:14.
[188] Ps. 103:4, (LXX).   [190] I Cor. 12:3.

or evil, and for this reason they need the Spirit's help.
Not even Gabriel could have announced events to come,[191]
unless the Spirit gave him foreknowledge — since one of
the gifts distributed by the Spirit is prophecy. Where did
the angel who interpreted the mysterious vision of Daniel,
the man of desires,[192] obtain the wisdom enabling him to
teach hidden things if not from the Holy Spirit? It is the
unique function of the Spirit to reveal mysteries, as it is
written, "God has revealed (them) to us through the
Spirit." [193] How can one explain the blessed life of thrones,
dominions, principalities, or powers,[194] if these spirits do
not behold the face of the Father who is in heaven? [195]
One cannot see the Father without the Spirit! It would be
like living in a house at night when the lamps are extin-
guished; one's eyes would be darkened and could not ex-
ercise their function. Unable to distinguish the value of
objects, one might very well treat gold as if it were iron.
It is the same in the spiritual world; it is impossible to
maintain a life of holiness without the Spirit. It would be
easier for an army to continue its maneuvers without a
general, or for a choir to sing on key without its director.
How can the Seraphim sing, "Holy, holy, holy," [196] without
the Spirit teaching them to constantly raise their voices
in praise? If all God's angels praise Him, and all His host,
they do so by cooperating with the Spirit. Do a thousand
thousands of angels serve Him? Do ten thousand times ten
thousand stand before Him? They accomplish their proper
work by the Spirit's power. All the indescribable harmony
of the heavenly realm, whether it be the praise of God
or the mutual concord of the bodiless powers, would be
impossible without the authority of the Spirit. Therefore
the Holy Spirit is present among those created beings which
are not gradually perfected, but are immediately perfect

---

[191] Lk. 1:11, 26ff.   [193] I Cor. 2:10.   [195] Cf. Mt. 18:10.
[192] Dan. 9:22ff, 10:10ff.   [194] Col. 1:16.   [196] Is. 6:3.

from the moment of their creation. He gives them His own grace, that their nature might be maintained in perfection.

39. But when we speak of the plan of salvation for men, accomplished in God's goodness by our great God and Savior Jesus Christ, who would deny that it was all made possible through the grace of the Spirit? Whether you wish to examine the Old Testament — the blessings of the patriarchs, the help given through the law, the types, the prophecies, the victories in battle, the miracles performed through righteous men — or everything that happened since the Lord's coming in the flesh, it all comes to pass through the Spirit. In the first place, the Lord was anointed with the Holy Spirit, who would henceforth be inseparably united to His very flesh, as it is written, "He on whom you see the Spirit descend and remain, this is He who . . . is my beloved Son," [197] and "God anointed Jesus of Nazareth with the Holy Spirit." [198] After His baptism, the Holy Spirit was present in every action He performed. He was there when the Lord was tempted by the devil: "Jesus was led up by the Spirit into the wilderness to be tempted." [199] The Spirit was united with Jesus when He performed miracles: "But if it is by the Spirit of God that I cast out demons . . ." [200] Nor did the Spirit leave Him after His resurrection from the dead. When the Lord renewed mankind by breathing into His Apostles' faces, (thus restoring the grace which Adam had lost, which God breathed into him in the beginning) what did He say? "Receive the Holy Spirit. If you forgive the sins of any, they are forgiven; if you retain the sins of any, they are retained." [201] Is it not indisputably clear that the Church is set in order by the Holy Spirit? "God has ap-

---

[197] Jn. 1:33, Mt. 3:17.   [199] Mt. 4:1.   [201] Jn. 20:22-23.
[198] Acts 10:30.   [200] Mt. 12:28.

pointed in the Church first apostles, second prophets, third teachers, then workers of miracles, then healers, helpers, administrators, speakers in various kinds of tongues." [202] This order is established according to the different gifts distributed by the Spirit.

40. Any intelligent man realizes that the work of the Holy Spirit will not cease, as some imagine, when the Lord makes His long-awaited return from heaven. On the contrary, the Holy Spirit will be present with Him on the day of His revelation, when He will judge the universe in righteousness as its only Ruler. Who is so ignorant of the good things which God has prepared for those who are worthy that he does not understand the crown of the righteous man is precisely the grace of the Spirit? On that Day spiritual glory shall be distributed in perfect abundance, as each receives a share proportionate to his uprightness. In the Father's house are many mansions,[203] meaning that some saints are of greater radiance and dignity than others: ". . . star differs from star in glory. So it is with the resurrection of the dead." [204] Those who were sealed by the Holy Spirit for the day of redemption, and have preserved pure and undiminished the fruits of the Spirit which they received, will hear the words, "Well done, good and faithful servant; you have been faithful over a little, I will set you over much." [205] Likewise, those who have grieved the Holy Spirit by their evil ways, or have not increased the talents they were given, will be deprived of what they received, and their share of grace will be given to others, or as one of the Gospels says, they will be completely cut to pieces,[206] meaning that they will be separated from the Spirit forever. It does not mean that the body is divided: one part handed over to punishment, and another

---

[202] I Cor. 12:28.   [204] I Cor. 15:41-42.
[203] Jn. 14:2.   [205] Mt. 25:21.   [206] Mt. 25:51.

part forgiven. The entire body has sinned, and God's righteous judgment is not like the old myths, where only part of the body is punished. Nor can the soul be cut in two, because sinful resolutions possess the soul completely, and accomplish evil with the body's cooperation. It is as I have said: the cutting to pieces is eternal separation of the soul from the Spirit. At present, before the day of judgment comes, even though the Spirit cannot dwell within those who are unworthy, He nevertheless is present in a limited way with those who have been baptized, hoping that their conversion will result in salvation. On the day of judgment, however, He will be completely cut off from the soul that has defiled His grace. That is why Scripture says that in hell no one confesses God and in death none can remember Him,[207] since the Spirit's help is no longer present. How can anyone imagine that the judgment will be accomplished without the Holy Spirit? Scripture says that He Himself is the reward of the righteous, on that day when the fulfillment is given instead of the promise, and sinners are deprived of what they once appeared to have. But the greatest proof that the Spirit is one with the Father and the Son is that He is said to have the same relationship to God as the spirit within us has to us: "For what person knows a man's thoughts except the spirit of the man which is in him? So also no one comprehends the thoughts of God except the Spirit of God.[208] Concerning this I have said enough.

---

[207] Ps. 6:6, (LXX).   [208] I Cor. 2:11.

CHAPTER 17. *Against those who say that the Holy*
Spirit must not be numbered with
the Father and the Son, but under
them. A summary of the correct
way of numbering them together.

41. It is by no means easy to understand what our
opponents mean by the term *subnumeration*. Everyone
knows that we borrowed this word from the language of
worldly wisdom, but now we must consider whether or
not it has any place in this discussion. We can learn from
experts in grammar that some nouns are common, used
to describe a great number of things, while others are more
specific, and the force of others is proper to one person
or thing. *Essence,* for example, is a common noun; it can
be used to describe all things, whether animate or inani-
mate. *Living* is more specific; it describes fewer subjects
than *essence*, but since it includes both rational and irra-
tional life, there are many more specific nouns: *human*
is more specific than *living*, and *man* is more specific than
human, while the individual names *Peter, James*, and *John*
are the most specific of all. Do they define subordination
as the division of the whole into lesser parts? I am unable
to believe that they have gone so utterly mad, treating the
God of all like a *thing* only to be perceived by the human
mind, having no real personal existence. They chop Him up
into subordinate pieces, and call this process *subnumeration!* Not even raving lunatics could suggest such a notion:
blasphemy notwithstanding, they are affirming exactly the
reverse of their original argument! Pieces of a whole cannot escape sharing the nature of the whole. This is so
obviously ridiculous that I am at a loss for words to answer
such nonsense; such depths of folly will spare them any

further attack. It would be like using a sword to cut through butter! Why should I exhaust my energy fighting such absurdity? All I want to do is to pass by such blasphemy in silence. But I love the brethren, and our opponents' stubbornness knows no bounds — so how can I possibly keep quiet?

42. Look at what they say; have you ever seen such arrogance? "We maintain that equal subjects are numbered together, but subordinate subjects should be given a lower ranking." Why do you say this? I cannot fathom your extraordinary wisdom. Do you mean that gold is placed at the head of the list, but because lead is cheaper, it must be placed further down? Is numerical rank such a powerful factor? Could it give lead the value of gold, or make gold cheap? In that case, we must list gold under precious stones, and make sure that smaller or duller stones receive lower numbers than larger or brighter ones. These men "spend their time in nothing except telling or hearing something new;" [209] what else can one expect from them? Let these champions of impiety be assigned numbers — the same as the Epicurean and Stoic philosophers! How is it possible to express higher and lower degrees of value by naming things in different order? If you have a copper coin and a gold coin, which is number one and which number two? They answer, "We do not claim to have two identical coins, but one of one type and one of another." But in what order will you name them? Each is mentioned at the same time. If you keep them separate, but assign each one the same number, you make them equal in value. On the other hand, if you combine them, they must be one in essence, since you place them in the same category. And what about adding them together? Suppose the person doing the arithmetic chooses the copper coin for his first figure?

[209] Acts 17:21.

Does that mean that the next figure must be smaller? I am
tired of refuting their ignorance; again, we must return
to the topic.

43.   Do you claim that the Son is numbered under the
Father, and the Spirit under the Son, or do you limit your
subordination to the Spirit alone? On the one hand, if
you consider the Son to be subordinate, you are reviving
the same old impiousness: that their essences are not the
same, that one is of less dignity than the other, that the
Son had a *beginning*, and by using that word you will again
stir up all the blasphemies against the Only-Begotten. I do
not have the time to again deny these errors; I have done
it elsewhere, and need not repeat it. On the other hand, if
you limit subordination to the Spirit alone, you must learn
once and for all that the Lord speaks of the Spirit and the
Father in exactly the same way: "In the name of the Father,
and of the Son, and of the Holy Spirit." [210] The words of
baptism are the same, and they declare that the relation of
the Spirit to the Son equals that of the Son with the Father.
If the Spirit is ranked with the Son, and the Son with the
Father, then the Spirit is obviously ranked with the Father
also. Their names are mentioned in one and the same
series; how can you speak of numbering *with* or numbering
under? Can numerical ranking ever change the nature of
anything? We use numbers to help distinguish various
things, but the things we number remain what they are by
nature and origin. Some material things we count, some we
measure, and others we weigh. Identical things we measure;
dissimilar things we count (unless the dissimilarity is so
fine that it must be measured). When the scales fall, heavy
objects are distinguished from light. These are convenient
means to determine various types of quantity, but no
amount of weighing, measuring, or counting can ever

[210] Mt. 28:19.

change a thing's nature. We can weigh gold or tin, but we would not claim that the *nature* of one is subordinate to the other on the basis of weight, and the same holds true for measure. Therefore we will use numbers as practical tools, and not claim that the very nature of a thing can be expressed with higher or lower ones! If such a principle of subordination is foreign to the created order, how dare anyone say the Spirit is subordinate? It is nothing but Greek sophistry to speak of inferior essences, degrees of rank, or subordination expressed with numbers.

CHAPTER 18. *How belief in three persons upholds the true doctrine of divine unity. Against those who subordinate the Spirit.*

44. When the Lord taught us the doctrine of Father, Son, and Holy Spirit, He did not make arithmetic a part of this gift! He did not say, "In the first, the second, and the third," or "In one, two, and three." He blessed us with the knowledge given us by faith, by means of holy Names. We are saved through faith; numbers have been invented as symbols of quantity. These men bring ruin on themselves through every possible source; they have even turned man's ability to count against the faith! Numbers cannot change the nature of anything, yet these men honor arithmetic more than the divine nature, lest they give the Paraclete more honor than He is due! But the Unapproachable One is beyond numbers, wisest sirs; imitate the reverence shown by the Hebrews of old to the unutterable name of God. Count if you must, but do not malign the truth. Either honor Him Who cannot be described with your silence, or number holy things in accord with true religion.

There is one God and Father, one Only-Begotten Son,
and one Holy Spirit. We declare each Person to be unique,
and if we must use numbers, we will not let a stupid arithmetic lead us astray to the idea of many gods.

45. If we count, we do *not* add, increasing from one
to many. We do not say, "one, two, three," or "first, second, and third." God says, "I am the first and I am the
last." [211] We have never to this present day heard of a
second God. We worship God from God, confessing the
uniqueness of the persons, while maintaining the unity of
the Monarchy. We do not divide divine knowledge and
scatter the pieces to the winds; we behold one Form (so
to speak) united by the invariableness of the Godhead,
present in God the Father and God the Only-Begotten.
The Son is in the Father and the Father in the Son; what
the Father is, the Son is likewise and vice-versa — such is
the unity. As unique Persons, they are one and one; as
sharing a common nature, both are one. How does one
and one not equal two Gods? Because we speak of the
emperor, and the emperor's image — but not two emperors.
The power is not divided, nor the glory separated. One is
the dominion and authority over us; we do not send up
glories to God, but glory; the honor given the image passes
to the prototype. The image of the emperor is an image by
imitation, but the Son is a natural image; in works of art
the likeness is dependent on its original form, and since
the divine nature is not composed of parts, union of the
persons is accomplished by partaking of the whole. The
Holy Spirit is one, and we speak of Him as unique, since
through the one Son He is joined to the Father. He com-
pletes the all-praised and blessed Trinity. He is not ranked
with the plurality of creation, but is described in the singular; this is sufficient evidence of His intimacy with the

---

[211] Is. 44:6.

Father and the Son. He is not one of many but one only: just as there is one Father and one Son, there is one Holy Spirit. Reason demands that the singular is separated from the plural or compound; therefore He does not share created nature. He is united to the Father and the Son as unit dwells with unit.

46. This is not our only proof that the Holy Spirit partakes of the fullness of divinity; the Spirit is described to be *of God*, not in the sense that all things are of God, but because He proceeds from the mouth of the Father, and is not begotten like the Son. Of course, the "mouth" of the Father is not a physical member, nor is the Spirit a dissipated exhalation, but "mouth" is used to the extent that it is appropriate to God, and the Spirit is the essence of life and divine sanctification. Their intimacy is made clear, while the ineffability of God's existence is safeguarded. He is also called the Spirit of Christ, since He is naturally related to Him. That is why Scripture says, "Anyone who does not have the Spirit of Christ does not belong to Him." [212] Only the Spirit can adequately glorify the Lord: "He will glorify me," [213] not as a creature, but as the Spirit of truth, since He Himself is truth shining brightly. He is the Spirit of wisdom, revealing Christ, the power of God and the wisdom of God, in His own greatness. As the Paraclete He reflects the goodness of the Paraclete (the Father) who sent Him, and His own dignity reveals the majesty of Him from Whom He proceeded. So on the one hand, there is a natural glory (as light is the glory of the sun), but on the other hand, there is a glory which chooses to bestow itself on those judged to be worthy. There are two types of the latter glory; the first is servile, offered by a creature to his superior: "A son honors his father, and a servant his master," [214] but the

---

[212] Rom. 8:9.   [213] Jn. 16:14.   [214] Mal. 1:6.

second is the glory shared by intimates, and it is this which
the Spirit fulfills. The Lord said of Himself: "I have glorified Thee on earth, having accomplished the work which
Thou gavest me to do," [215] and concerning the Spirit He
said, "He will glorify me, for He will take what is mine
and declare it to you." [216] The Son is also glorified by the
Father, when the Father says, "I have glorified Thee, and
I will glorify Thee again." [217] The Spirit is glorified by
His communion with the Father and the Son, and by the
testimony of the Only-Begotten: "Every sin and blasphemy
will be forgiven men: but the blasphemy against the Spirit
will not be forgiven." [218]

47.   If we are illumined by divine power, and fix our
eyes on the beauty of the image of the invisible God, and
through the image are led up to the indescribable beauty
of its source, it is because we have been inseparably joined
to the Spirit of knowledge. He gives those who love the
vision of truth the power which enables them to see the
image, and this power is Himself. He does not reveal it
to them from outside sources, but leads them to knowledge
personally, "No one knows the Father except the Son," [219]
and "No one can say 'Jesus is Lord' except in the Holy
Spirit." [220] Notice that it does not say *through* the Spirit,
but *in* the Spirit. It also says, "God is Spirit, and those who
worship Him must worship in spirit and truth," [221] and
"in Thy light do we see light," [222] through the illumination
of the Holy Spirit, "the true light that enlightens every
man that comes into the world." [223] He reveals the glory
of the Only-Begotten in Himself, and He gives true worshippers the knowledge of God in Himself. The way to
divine knowledge ascends from one Spirit through the one

---

[215] Jn. 17:4.   [218] Mt. 12:32.   [221] Jn. 4:24.
[216] Jn. 16:14.   [219] Mt. 11:27.   [222] Ps. 36:9.
[217] Cf. Jn. 12:28.   [220] I Cor. 12:3.   [223] Jn. 1:9.

Son to the one Father. Likewise, natural goodness, inherent holiness and royal dignity reaches from the Father through the Only-Begotten to the Spirit. Thus, we do not lose the true doctrine of one God by confessing the persons. Those who teach subordination, and talk about first, second, and third, ought to realize that they are introducing erroneous Greek polytheism into pure Christian theology. This evil invention of subordinationism can result in nothing except a first, second, and third God. We will be content with the order established by the Lord. He who confuses this order is as guilty of transgressing the law as an impious blasphemer. Enough has been said to undo their error; subordination cannot be used to describe persons who share the same nature. But we cannot resist one final blow to our contentious and feeble-minded enemy. Let us assume, for a moment, that anything labeled "number two" is subordinate to "number one." But what do we find written? "The *first* man was from the earth, a man of dust; the *second* man is from heaven." [224] Again, "But it is not the spiritual which is first, but the physical, and then the spiritual." [225] If the second is subordinate to the first, and since what is subordinate is always inferior to that to which it is subordinated, according to you, then, the spiritual is inferior to the physical, and the man from heaven is inferior to the man of dust!

CHAPTER 19. *Against those who say that the Spirit should not be glorified.*

48. "Even if this is true," they answer, "glory should not be given to the Spirit to such an extreme that we must

---

[224] I Cor. 15:47.   [225] I Cor. 15:46.

sing Him doxologies." But from where do we obtain testimony of the Spirit's ineffable dignity, if not from His communion with the Father and the Son? Our opponents will not recognize this evidence as trustworthy. If we ponder the meaning of His name, and the greatness of His deeds, and the multitude of blessings He has showered on us and on all creation, it is possible for us to understand at least partially the greatness of His nature and unapproachable power. He is named Spirit: "God is Spirit," [226] and "the Spirit of our nostrils, the Lord's Anointed." [227] He is called holy, as the Father is holy and the Son is holy. For creatures, holiness comes from without; for the Spirit, holiness fills His very nature. He is not sanctified, but sanctifies. He is called good, as the Father is good; the essence of the Spirit embraces the goodness of the Father. He is called upright – the Lord my God is upright [228] – because He is truth and righteousness personified. He does not lean to one side or the other since His nature is changeless. He shares the name Paraclete with the Only-Begotten, who said, "I will ask the Father, and He will give you another Paraclete." [229] The Spirit shares titles held in common by the Father and the Son; He receives these titles due to His natural and intimate relationship with them. Where else would they come from? Again He is called the ruling Spirit,[230] the Spirit of truth, and the Spirit of wisdom. It is written that "the Spirit of God has made me," [231] and that "God filled Bezaleel with the divine Spirit of wisdom, understanding, and knowledge." [232] Titles like these are great and lofty, but they do not exhaust His glory.

49. What does the Spirit do? His works are ineffable in majesty, and innumerable in quantity. How can we even

---

[226] Jn. 4:24. [229] Jn. 14:16. [231] Job 33:4.
[227] Lam. 4:20, (LXX).[230] Cf. Ps. 50:10, (LXX).[232] Ex. 31:3, (LXX).
[228] Cf. Ps. 92:15.

ponder what extends beyond the ages? What did He do before creation began? How great are the graces He showered on creation? What power will He wield in the age to come? He existed; He pre-existed; He co-existed with the Father and the Son before the ages. Even if you can imagine anything beyond the ages, you will discover that the Spirit is even further beyond. If you consider creation, remember that the heavenly powers were established by the Spirit; [233] this establishment means that they were disinclined to fall away from good. The Spirit enables the heavenly powers to avoid evil, and persevere in goodness. Christ comes, and the Spirit prepares His way. He comes in the flesh, but the Spirit is never separated from Him. Working of miracles and gifts of healing come from the Holy Spirit. Demons are driven out by the Spirit of God. The presence of the Spirit despoils the devil. Remission of sins is given through the gift of the Spirit: "You were washed, you were sanctified ... in the name of the Lord Jesus Christ and in the Holy Spirit of our God." [234] Through the Spirit we become intimate with God: "God has sent the Spirit of His Son into our hearts, crying, 'Abba! Father!' " [235] Resurrection from the dead is accomplished by the operation of the Spirit: "Thou sendest forth Thy Spirit, and they are created; and Thou renewest the face of the earth." [236] If "creation" means bringing the dead back to life, how great the work of the Spirit is! He gives us risen life, refashioning our souls in the spiritual life. On the other hand, if "creation" means the conversion of sinners to a better way of life (the Scripture often understands it this way; for example, the words of Paul: "If any one is in Christ, he is a new creation." [237]), and the renewal of this earthly life, and changing our earthly, passionate life into heavenly citizenship, then we should

---

[233] Ps. 32:6, (LXX).   [235] Gal. 4:6.   [237] II Cor. 5:17.
[234] I Cor. 6:11.   [236] Ps. 104:30.

know that our souls attain such a high degree of exaltation through the Spirit. Understanding all this, how can we be afraid of giving the Spirit too much honor? We should instead fear that even though we ascribe to Him the highest titles we can devise or our tongues pronounce, our ideas about Him might still fall short. The Spirit speaks with the authority of the Lord: "The Spirit said to him (Peter) 'Rise and go down, and accompany them without hesitation; for I have sent them.'" [238] Are these the words of an abject inferior? "Set apart for me Barnabas and Saul for the work to which I have called them." [239] Does a slave give commands like this? Isaiah says, "The Lord God and His Spirit have sent me," [240] and "the Spirit came down from the Lord and led them." [241] Do not try to again convince me that this "leading" by the Spirit is some lowly service. Scripture testifies that it is the work of God: "He led forth His people like sheep," [242] it says, and "Thou who leadest Joseph like a flock," [243] and "He led them in safety, so that they were not afraid." [244] Therefore, when you hear that "the Comforter will bring to remembrance all that I have said to you, and will guide you into all truth," [245] do not quibble over the meaning.

50. Scripture also says that "the Spirit Himself intercedes for us." [246] Our opponents conclude that since an intercessor must always be inferior to a benefactor, the Spirit must therefore be inferior to God. Have you never heard what Scripture says concerning the Only-Begotten? "He is at the right hand of God, and intercedes for us." [247] Do not deprive Him of the faith and praise He is due. He has been within you; have you expelled Him? He

---

[238] Acts 10:20.   [242] Ps. 78:52.   [246] Rom. 8:26.
[239] Acts 13:2.   [243] Ps. 80:1.   [247] Cf. Rom. 8:34.
[240] Is. 48:16.   [244] Ps. 78:53.
[241] Is. 63:14, (LXX).   [245] Jn. 14:26; 16:13.

teaches us who formerly were blind; He guides us to choose what is good. Do not repay your benefactor's love for man with ingratitude; that would be the height of baseness. Do not grieve the Holy Spirit of God.[248] Listen to what Stephen, the first martyr, says when he rebukes the people for their insubordination and disobedience: "You always resist the Holy Spirit." [249] Isaiah says, "they rebelled and grieved His Holy Spirit; therefore He turned to be their enemy." [250] In another place it says, "The house of Jacob angered the Spirit of the Lord." [251] Do these passages not demonstrate the authority of His might? I will leave it to my readers to judge how these passages ought to be interpreted. Are we to regard the Spirit as an instrument, a servant to be ranked with other creatures, a fellow slave? Or should even the slightest whisper of this blasphemy grieve pious ears? Do you call the Spirit a slave? But "the slave does not know what his master is doing," [252] and, "what person knows a man's thoughts except the spirit of the man which is in him? So also no one comprehends the thoughts of God except the Spirit of God." [253]

CHAPTER 20. *Against those who claim that the Spirit should not be ranked as a master or a slave, but as a freeman.*

51. Some say that the Spirit is neither master nor slave, but like a freeman. What miserable nonsense; what pitiful audacity! Which shall I lament, their ignorance or their blasphemy? They insult the dogmas pertaining to the

---

[248] Eph. 4:30.　　[250] Is. 63:10.　　[252] Jn. 15:15.
[249] Acts 7:51.　　[251] Micah 2:7, (LXX).　　[253] I Cor. 2:11.

divine nature by confining them within human categories.
They think they see differences of dignity among men, and
then apply such variation to the ineffable nature of God.
Do they not realize that even among men, no one is a
slave by nature? Men are brought under the yoke of slavery
either because they are captured in battle or else they sell
themselves into slavery due to poverty, as the Egyptians
became the slaves of Pharaoh. Sometimes, by a wise and
inscrutable providence, worthless children are commanded
by their father to serve their more intelligent brothers and
sisters. (Any upright person investigating the circumstances
would realize that such situations bring much benefit, and
are not a sentence of condemnation for those involved.
It is better for a man who lacks intelligence and self-
control to become another's possession. Governed by his
master's intelligence, he will become like a chariot driven
by a skilled horseman, or a ship with a seasoned sailor at
the tiller.) That is why Jacob obtained his father's blessing, and became Esau's lord: [254] so that this foolish son,
who had no intelligence to properly guide him, might profit
from his prudent brother, even against his will. Canaan
became "a slave of slaves to his brothers," [255] because his
father Ham was void of understanding, unable to teach his
son any virtue. That is why men become slaves, but those
who escape poverty, war, or the need of a guardian, are
free. And even though one man is called a master, and
another a slave, we are all the possessions of our Creator;
we all share the rank of slave. Who is free from bondage
in the world beyond? As soon as the angels were created,
they began to serve. The heavenly hosts do not greedily
desire to rule each other; they all bow before God, fearing
Him as their Master, and glorifying Him as Creator.
"A son honors his father, and a servant his master." [256]
God demands one or the other from all: "If then I am

---

[254] Cf. Gen. 27:29.   [255] Gen. 9:25.   [256] Mal. 1:6.

a father, where is my honor? And if I am a master, where
is my fear?" [257] Our lives would be most pitiful if they
were not under a master's oversight; we would resemble
the apostate angels, who stiffened their necks against
Almighty God, and refused to serve Him. Their nature
was the same as their obedient fellow servants, yet they
chose to disobey their Creator. So whom will you call
a freeman? Someone who serves no King? Someone who
lacks both the strength to rule, or the willingness to be
ruled? No such nature exists, and it is blasphemous to
think that the Spirit is such a being. Either He is a creature,
and therefore a slave, or else He is above creation, and
shares the Kingship.

CHAPTER 21. *Scriptural testimony that*
the Spirit is called Lord.

52. Why fight with such trifling arguments, and win
such a shameful victory, when we can indisputably prove
the excellence of the Spirit's glory? If we repeat what we
have learned from Scripture, every one of these Spirit-fight-
ers (Pneumatomachoi) will raise a loud and vehement
outcry, stop their ears, pick up stones or any other weapon
at hand, and charge against us. But we must care about
truth, not our own safety. We have discovered the meaning
of the Apostle's words: "May the Lord direct your hearts
to the love of God and to the steadfastness of Christ." [258]
Who is this Lord who directs us into the love of God, and
into the patient endurance of Christ, that we may over-
come our tribulations? They want to make the Spirit a
slave; let them answer this one: If the subject of this pas-

---

[257] Idem.   [258] II Thess. 3:5.

sage is God the Father, it certainly would have said, "May
the Lord direct your hearts *to His own love*; if it were the
Son, it would add "and to His own steadfastness." Who
else worthy to be honored with the title "Lord" can they
find? Here is another passage similar to the preceding
one: "May the Lord make you increase and abound in love
to one another and to all men, as we do to you, so that
He may establish your hearts unblameable in holiness
before our God and Father, at the coming of our Lord
Jesus with all His saints." [259] Which Lord is Paul entreating
to establish the hearts of the Thessalonian faithful unblameable in holiness before our God and Father, at the
coming of our Lord? Our opponents place the Holy Spirit
among the ministering spirits sent forth to serve; can they
answer our question? No, they cannot. Let them listen
to even more testimony of the Spirit's Lordship: "Now
the Lord is the Spirit" [260] and "this comes from the Lord
who is the Spirit." [261] But to leave no room for further
doubt, I will quote the Apostle's words in greater detail:
"To this day, when they read the Old Testament, that
same veil remains unlifted, because only through Christ
is it taken away . . . when a man turns to the Lord the veil
is removed. Now the Lord is the Spirit . . ." [262] Why does
Paul say this? Because someone who adheres to the bare
letter of the law, and busies himself with legal observances,
has veiled his own heart with Jewish interpretation of
the law. Such a person is ignorant that the bodily observ-
ance of the law has been abrogated by the coming of
Christ, and the types have been exchanged for the truth.
Lamps are not needed after sunrise, and since the truth
has appeared, the job of the law is over, and the prophets
become silent. On the other hand, someone given the
ability to perceive the depth of the law's meaning, who

---

[259] I Thess. 3:12-13.   [261] II Cor. 3:18.
[260] II Cor. 3:17.   [262] II Cor. 3:14, 16-17.

passes through the curtain of literal obscurity and arrives at unutterable truths, is like Moses, who removed his veil when he spoke with God. Such a man has turned from the letter to the Spirit. The veil on Moses' face is analogous to the obscurity of the instruction offered by the law, just as spiritual contemplation corresponds to Moses speaking to the Lord with face unveiled. He who throws away the letter and turns to the Lord when reading the law (and now the Lord is called Spirit) becomes like Moses, whose face shone with the glory of God's manifestation. Objects placed near something brilliantly colored themselves become tinted through reflected light; likewise he who fixes his gaze on the Spirit is transfigured to greater brightness, his heart illumined by the light of the Spirit's truth. Then the glory of the Spirit is changed into such a person's own glory, not stingily, or dimly, but with the abundance we would expect to find within someone who had been enlightened by the Spirit. Are you not ashamed, my opponent, when you hear the Apostle's words: "You are God's temple and God's Spirit dwells in you"? [263] Is a slave's house honored with the title of temple? How can someone who calls Scripture "God-inspired" (since it was written under the inspiration of the Holy Spirit) use language that insults and belittles Him?

CHAPTER 22. *Like the Father and the Son, the Spirit is incomprehensible, since He partakes of the same nature.*

53. We can learn about the loftiness of the Spirit's nature not only because He shares the same titles and

---

[263] I Cor. 3:16.

works as the Father and the Son, but also because He, like them, cannot be grasped by our thoughts. The Lord says that the Father is beyond human conception, and that the same is true of Himself, the Son. Concerning the Father He says: "O righteous Father, the world has not known Thee." [264] By the world He does not mean the whole complex of heaven and earth, but this life of ours, subject to death and endless troubles. Concerning Himself He says: "Yet a little while, and the world will see me no more, but you will see me." [265] Again, by "world" He means those who are tied down by a material and carnal life, and restrict truth to what is seen by their eyes. They refuse to believe in the resurrection, and become unable to see the Lord with the eyes of their hearts. So neither the Father nor the Son may be seen by the "world," but notice that He uses the same language concerning the Spirit: "the Spirit of truth, whom the world cannot receive, because it neither sees Him nor knows Him; you know Him, for He dwells with you, and will be in you." [266] A carnal man's mind is not trained in contemplation, but remains buried in the mud of fleshly lusts, powerless to look up and see the spiritual light of the truth. So the "world" — life enslaved by carnal passions — can no more receive the grace of the Spirit than a weak eye can look at the light of a sunbeam. First the Lord cleansed His disciples' lives through His teaching, and then He gave them the ability to both see and contemplate the Spirit. He says, "You are already made clean by the word which I have spoken to you." [267] Therefore, "the world cannot receive Him, because it neither sees Him nor knows Him; you know Him, for He dwells with you." [268] Isaiah says, "Thus saith the Lord God, . . . who settled the earth and the things in it; and gives breath to the people on it, and

---

[264] Jn. 17:25.   [266] Jn. 14:17.   [268] Jn. 14:17.
[265] Jn. 14:19.   [267] Jn. 15:3.

Spirit to those who tread on it;" [269] from this we can learn that those who trample earthly things and rise above them become worthy to receive the gift of the Holy Spirit. What should we think about Him? The world cannot receive Him, and only holy men can contemplate Him through purity of heart. Is there any limit to the honor He deserves?

CHAPTER 23. *The Spirit is glorified through the recounting of His unique wonders.*

54. We believe that the Spirit is present everywhere, while the rest of the bodiless powers are circumscribed by place. The angel who came to Cornelius [270] was not with Philip at the same time,[271] nor did the angel who spoke with Zechariah from the right side of the altar [272] simultaneously occupy his place in heaven. But the Spirit is believed to have been inspiring Habakkuk and Daniel in Babylon at the same time, though they were in different places; [273] the same is true for Jeremiah in the dungeon [274] and Ezekiel by the river Chebar.[275] "The Spirit of the Lord fills the world;" [276] "where shall I go from Thy Spirit or where shall I flee from Thy presence?" [277] The prophet says: "I am with you, says the Lord of hosts ... My Spirit abides among you." [278] If wherever God is, the Spirit is present also, what nature shall we presume Him to have? An all-encompassing nature, or a

[269] Is. 42:5, (LXX).   [273] Cf. Dan. 14:33ff, (LXX).   [276] Wis. 1:7.
[270] Acts 10:3.   [274] Jer. 20:2, (LXX).   [277] Ps. 139:7.
[271] Acts 8:26.   [275] Ez. 1:1.   [278] Hag. 2:4-5.
[272] Luke 1:11.

nature confined to particular places, as we have described the nature of the angels? No one would say the latter. He is divine in nature, infinite in greatness, mighty in His works, good in His blessings; shall we not exalt Him; shall we not glorify Him? I reckon that this "glorifying" is nothing else but the recounting of His own wonders. Our opponents' argument would force us to never even mention the blessings which flow from Him to us. Obviously this is absurd, so the opposite is true: to describe His wonders gives Him the fullest glorification possible. The same is true for the God and Father of our Lord Christ and the Only-Begotten Son Himself; we are only able to glorify them by recounting their wonders to the best of our ability.

CHAPTER 24. *Considering that many created things are glorified proves the absurdity of refusing to glorify the Spirit.*

55. An ordinary man is said to be crowned with glory and honor;[279] it is also promised that glory and honor and peace are in store for everyone who does good.[280] Israel's glory is unique for to it belongs the sonship, the glory, and the worship.[281] The Psalmist speaks of his own personal glory: "that my glory may praise Thee;"[282] and "awake, my glory!"[283] St. Paul says there is one glory of the sun, and another glory of the moon, and another glory of the stars[284] and that the dispensation of death (the law of Moses) was glorious, but the dispensation of the Spirit

---

[279] Ps. 8:5.   [281] Rom. 9:4.   [283] Ps. 56:8, (LXX).
[280] Rom. 2:10.   [282] Ps. 30:12.   [284] I Cor. 15:41.

is even more glorious.[285] So many things are glorified; do you wish the Spirit alone to be deprived of glory? How can He possibly not deserve glorification? The Psalms say that a righteous man's glory will be great; how can you say that the Spirit has no glory at all? Is it not obvious that we will inescapably bring sin upon ourselves by persisting in these arguments? If a man is being saved through righteous works, he glorifies God-fearing men; do you suppose such a man would deprive the Spirit of the glory He deserves?

Now it is true that some of them are willing to glorify the Spirit, but not with the Father and the Son. But the Lord has assigned the Spirit His proper place; why should we forsake it to invent another place? He is always described as united with the Godhead; why should He be deprived of His glory? We hear His name in the creed, at saving baptism, in the working of miracles. He takes up His abode in the saints; He bestows grace on the obedient. No gift can be bestowed on creation unless the Holy Spirit gives it; not even a single word can be spoken in defense of Christ unless the Holy Spirit inspires it — as we have learned in the Gospels from our Lord and Savior.[286] How could anyone who has partaken of the Holy Spirit be willing to forget or disregard that He is united to the Father and the Son in every way and try to tear Him away from them? Where will you take Him to be ranked? Among creatures? But all creation is in bondage and the Spirit frees it; "where the Spirit of the Lord is, there is freedom." [287] There are many other arguments why the Holy Spirit cannot be counted as a created nature, but for the moment I will not speak of them. If I were to use all the evidence already available to us in a manner suitable for the loftiness of this discussion, our opponents' objections would be overthrown, but such an enormous treatise would

---

[285] Cf. II Cor. 3:7ff.   [286] Mt. 10:19-20.   [287] II Cor. 3:17.

result that my readers would be exhausted by its length. I will reserve these arguments for a special book, and concern myself with the following points.

56. Let us examine these points one by one: The Spirit is good by nature, as the Father and the Son are good, but the creature wishing to share goodness must choose to do so. The Spirit searches even the depths of God,[288] but the creature receives enlightenment concerning ineffable truths through the Spirit. He gives life together with the Father who enlivens all things, and with the life-giving Son: "If the Spirit of Him who raised Jesus from the dead dwells in you, He who raised Christ Jesus from the dead will give life to your mortal bodies also through His Spirit which dwells in you." [289] Also, "My sheep hear my voice . . . and I give them eternal life." [290] But the Spirit gives life in the same way: "the Spirit is life because of righteousness." [291] The Lord testifies that "the Spirit gives life; the flesh profits nothing." [292] How can we separate the Spirit from His life-giving power and associate Him with things which by nature are lifeless? Who is so perverse; who is so devoid of the heavenly gift, so unnourished by God's good words; who is so empty of sharing eternal hopes, that he would separate the Spirit from the Godhead, and number Him among creatures?

57. Others say that the Spirit is in us as a gift from God, and a gift is not to be given the same honor as the giver. The Spirit is God's gift, but He is the gift of life ("the law of the Spirit of life in Christ Jesus has set me free . . ." [293]) and a gift of power ("you shall receive power when the Holy Spirit has come upon you").[294] You

[288] I Cor. 2:10.   [291] Rom. 8:10.   [293] Rom. 8:2.
[289] Rom. 8:11.   [292] Jn. 6:63.   [294] Acts 1:8.
[290] Jn. 10:27-28.

hold the Spirit in contempt because He is a gift? Did not
God give His Son as a gift to mankind as well? "He who
did not spare His own Son but gave Him up for us all,
will He not also give us all things with Him?" [295] Also,
"we have received . . . the Spirit which is from God, that
we might understand the gifts bestowed on us by God," [296]
gifts meaning here the mystery of the Incarnation. Those
who maintain this opinion turn God's immeasurable loving-
kindness into an occasion of blasphemy; really, they sur-
pass the ingratitude of the Jews! The Spirit gives us the
freedom to call God our Father, and they find fault with
Him! "God has sent the Spirit of His Son into our hearts
crying, 'Abba! Father!' " [297] so that the Spirit's cry might
become the same cry of all those who receive Him.

CHAPTER 25. *The preposition* in *or* by *is used
the same way as* with; *and also has
the same force as* with.

58. "How is it," our opponents ask, "that Scripture
nowhere describes the Spirit to be glorified together with
the Father and the Son?" It carefully avoids the phrase
with the Spirit, but always prefers *in the Spirit* as a more
suitable expression to use when ascribing glory to God.
For my own part, I cannot agree that *in* (or *by*) and
with are used to express degrees of dignity; *in* may easily
express a dignity just as lofty. There are many instances
where *in* is used, but *with* is actually signified, for instance,
it actually says "I will go into thine house *in* burnt offerings
(ἐν ὁλοκαυτώμασιν)" [298] but we would say *with* burnt

---

[295] Rom. 8:32.   [297] Gal. 4:6.
[296] I Cor. 2:12.   [298] Ps. 65:13, (LXX).

offerings. Similarly it says, "He brought them out *in* silver and gold," [299] and "Thou wilt not go forth *in* our armies." [300] In both cases *in* really means *with*. There are endless examples of this. But I would very much like to know, according to this newly-discovered wisdom, if the Apostle used *in* to ascribe glory — since that is how our opponents interpret Scripture. I cannot find anywhere the formula "Glory and honor to Thee, O Father, *through* Thine Only-Begotten Son, *in* (or by) the Holy Spirit," yet our opponents use this formula with the same ease as they breathe air. You can find each of these clauses separately, but they are not combined in a doxology this way. If our opponents insist on exact conformity to the Scriptures they have better provide references. If they claim that this doxology has become customary, they cannot forbid our doxology on the grounds of custom.

59.   Both doxologies are used by the faithful, and so we use both; we believe that either one ascribes perfect glory to the Spirit. The mouths of these corrupters of the truth may be more easily silenced, however, by Scripture's identical use of the conjunction *and* and the preposition *with*. Our opponents have no weapon against this argument, and so they are left wide open for our attack. "Paul, *and* Silvanus, *and* Timothy" [301] means exactly the same as Paul, *with* Timothy, *and* Silvanus; either expression preserves the combination of names. The Lord said ". . . the Father *and* the Son *and* the Holy Spirit;" [302] if I would say "the Father *and* the Son *with* the Holy Spirit," have I changed the meaning of anything? There are many instances of the conjunction *and* being used to connect a series of names: "The grace of the Lord Jesus Christ, *and* the love of God *and* the fellowship of the Holy Spirit," [303] or

---

[299] Ps. 104:37, (LXX).   [301] I Thess. 1:1.   [303] II Cor. 13:14.
[300] Ps. 43:9, (LXX).   [302] Cf. Mt. 28:19.

"I appeal to you, brethren, by our Lord Jesus Christ *and* by the love of the Spirit." [304] If we were to substitute *with* for every *and* in the above passages, what difference would it make? I cannot see any, unless a pedantic grammarian insists that a coordinate conjunction brings about a stronger union that a preposition. Even if this were so, we would not need a lengthy argument to defend ourselves concerning this point. They are not *really* concerned with syllables or various usages of words, but with defending a position radically different in authority and truth from our own. It really makes little difference which syllables are used, but they would like to canonize some, and exclude others from the Church! I will explain why our fathers began to use the preposition *with* in the doxology, although it seems to me that the reason is obvious even to someone hearing it for the first time. *With* and *and* would be equally useful in fighting the wickedness of Sabellius, since either one reveals that the Persons are distinct: "I *and* my Father will come," [305] or "I *and* the Father are one." [306] But *with* is an especially useful word because it testifies to eternal communion and unceasing cooperation. If we say that the Son is *with* the Father, we mean two things: first, that their persons are distinct, and second, that they are inseparably united in fellowship. We can observe the same thing in human affairs: *and* indicates that an action is performed by more than one person, but *with* reveals the fellowship among the persons more explicitly. For instance, if we hear that Paul *and* Timothy sailed to Macedonia, or Tychicus *and* Onesimus were sent to the Colossians, we know that each pair accomplished a certain action. But if we were told that they sailed *with* each other, or that one was sent *with* the other, we would learn in addition that they accomplished the action *in common*. So not only does the word *with* destroy the heresy of Sabellius, as no other

[304] Rom. 15:30.   [305] Cf. Jn. 14:23.   [306] Jn. 10:30.

word can, but it also defeats those who err in the opposite
direction. I am referring to those who use intervals of time
to separate the Son from the Father, saying there was a
time when the Son was not, or the Spirit from the Son,
calling the Spirit a created being.

60. As far as the differences between *in* and *with*
are concerned, they are as follows: *with* demonstrates
that persons mutually share a common act, for example,
sailing *with*, or living in the same house *with*, or doing
anything else in common. *In* refers to their relationship
to the place or thing in which the action is performed. No
sooner than we hear the words "they sailed in . . ." or
"they live in . . ." we immediately picture a boat or a
house. This is the normal difference between these two
words in ordinary usage; if we wished to be industrious we
could discover many more examples, but I have no more
time to analyze syllables. I have demonstrated that union
is most clearly signified by the term *with*; declare a truce
and place this word under safe conduct, if you will; stop
your savage and incessant war against it. Even though
this term is the most precise, if someone wishes to join
the names in the doxology with the word *and* (as the Gospel does and as we do in baptism: Father *and* Son *and*
Holy Spirit), let him do it; no one will object. If you wish,
these could be the terms of the treaty. But our opponents
would rather have their tongues cut out than even accept
the word *and*; it is this word that rouses them to war
against us. They insist we must give glory to God *in* the
Holy Spirit, but never *and to* the Holy Spirit, passionately
clutching this one word as if it contained power to lower
the Spirit. Perhaps it would be best if we speak at greater
length concerning this word. When they have heard what
we have to say, I will be very much surprised if they do
not recognize that this little word has betrayed them, deserting to the side of the Spirit's glory.

CHAPTER 26. *There are many ways in* may be
*suitably used in reference to
the Spirit.*

61. Although *in* is a short and simple word, it seems
to me that it is used in a multitude of various ways. We
shall discover, however, that all these usages are appropriate when applied to the Spirit. We say, for instance, that
form abides *in* matter, or that power dwells *in* its recipient,
or a certain habit affects a person *in* whom it makes its
home, and so on. Therefore, since the Holy Spirit perfects
reason-endowed beings, He is present *in* them in the same
way form is present *in* matter. Such a person no longer
lives according to the flesh, but is led by the Spirit of God.
He is called a son of God, because he is conformed to the
image of the Son of God; we call him a spiritual man.
The ability to see is *in* a healthy eye; likewise the Spirit is
working *in* a purified soul: Paul prays that the Ephesians'
eyes might be enlightened by the Spirit of wisdom.[307]
Artistic skill dwells *in* the artist and the grace of the Spirit
is always present *in* its recipient, even if the grace is not
perpetually in operation. The artist's skill exists as potential within him; only if he works is the potential acti-
vated. The Spirit is continually present with those who are
worthy, but actively works as He is needed, whether in
prophecy, or healings, or other wonderful works. There
are changeable factors *in* our bodies, such as health or
fever, and the Spirit's presence in our souls is comparable,
since He will not stay with those whose wills are un-
stable. Such people have no perseverance, and drive away
the grace they have received. Consider the example of Saul
(from whom the Spirit of the Lord departed),[308] or the

---

[307] Eph. 1:17.   [308] Cf. I Sam. 16:14.

seventy elders of the children of Israel (with the exception
of Eldad and Medad, the only ones with whom the Spirit
remained),[309] or anyone else similar to these in conduct.
Again, the working of the Holy Spirit is similar to the
action of reason within our souls, which sometimes moves
our hearts to think, and at other times moves our tongues
to speak, since the Spirit Himself bears witness with our
spirit, and cries in our hearts, "Abba! Father!" [310] At other
times He speaks on our behalf, as when it says: "it is not
you who speak, but the Spirit of the Father speaking
through you." [311] Again, when we consider the distribution
of gifts, we perceive that the Spirit is a whole divided into
parts, since we are all members one of another, having
gifts that differ according to the grace given to us.[312] The
eye cannot say to the hand, "I have no need of you," or
again the head to the feet, "I have no need of you," [313]
but all the members complete the body of Christ in the
unity of the Spirit, each member assisting the others with
aid provided by the unique gifts it has received. God arranged the organs in the body, each one of them, as He
chose,[314] so that the members may have the same care for
one another, since from the beginning they are spiritually
united in sympathy. "If one member suffers, all suffer together; if one member is honored, all rejoice together." [315]
We live in the Spirit as individual members of a body,
because we were all baptized into one Spirit, in one body.[316]

62. Although paradoxical, it is nevertheless true that
Scripture frequently speaks of the Spirit in terms of
place — a place *in* which people are made holy. We shall
demonstrate that even this figure of speech does not down-
grade the Spirit; rather, it glorifies Him. Words which

---

[309] Cf. Num. 11:26 ff.   [312] Rom. 12:6-7.   [315] I Cor. 12:25, 26.
[310] Rom. 8:16, 15.   [313] I Cor. 13:21.   [316] Cf. I Cor. 12:13.
[311] Mt. 10:20.   [314] I Cor. 12:18.

normally have a physical meaning are frequently transposed to a spiritual plane by Scripture, for the sake of clarity. For example, the Psalmist says, "Be to me a protecting God, and a place of strength to save me,"[317] and in reference to the Spirit God says, "Behold, there is a place by Me: thou shalt stand upon the rock."[318] This "place" is contemplation in the Spirit, and when Moses entered this "place" God revealed Himself to him. Only in this special "place" can true worship be offered. The Law said, "Take heed that you do not offer your burnt offerings at every place that you see, but at the place which the Lord shall choose . . ."[319] But what is a *spiritual* burnt offering, but the sacrifice of praise? Where can we offer it? Only *in* the Holy Spirit! Where did we learn this? From the Lord Himself: The true worshippers will worship the Father in Spirit and in truth.[320] Jacob saw this "place" and said, "The Lord is in this place."[321] The Spirit is indeed the dwelling-place of the saints, and the saint is a suitable abode for the Spirit, since he has supplied God with a house, and is called a temple of God. Similarly, Paul speaks *in* Christ; he says, "in the sight of God we speak *in* Christ,"[322] and Christ speaks in Paul: "You desire proof that Christ is speaking *in* me."[323] The same Paul utters mysteries *in* the Spirit,[324] and the Spirit also speaks *in* Paul.

63. The Spirit is said to dwell *in* created things in many and various ways, but as far as His relationship to the Father and the Son is concerned, it is more appropriate to say that He dwells *with* them, rather than *in* them. Those who are worthy receive His grace, and He works with*in* them. However, we cannot contemplate His pre-eternal

---

[317] Ps. 70:3, (LXX).
[318] Ex. 33:21, (LXX).
[319] Deut. 12:13-14.
[320] Cf. Jn. 4:23.
[321] Gen. 28:16.
[322] II Cor. 2:17.
[323] II Cor. 3:13.
[324] I Cor. 14:2.

existence and permanent presence with the Son and the
Father unless we search for words which suitably express
such an everlasting union. Truly precise *co-existence* can
only be predicated of things which are mutually inseparable. For example, we would say that heat exists *in* red-hot
iron, but co-exists *with* fire, or that health is present *in*
the body, but life co-exists *with* the soul. Whenever the
union between things is intimate, natural, and inseparable,
it is more appropriate to use *with* since this word suggests
an indivisible union. On the other hand, in situations where
the grace of the Spirit comes and goes, it is more proper
to say that the Spirit exists *in* someone, even in the case
of well-disposed persons with whom He abides continually.
Therefore, when we consider the Spirit's *rank*, we think
of Him as present *with* the Father and the Son, but when
we consider the working of His grace on its recipients, we
say that the Spirit is *in* us. If we say, "Glory to the Father
through the Son *in* the Holy Spirit," we are not describing
the Spirit's rank, but confessing our own weakness, since
we show that we are not capable of glorifying God on
our own; only *in* the Spirit is this made possible. In Him
we are able to thank God for the blessings we have received. To the extent that we are purified from evil, each
receives a smaller or a larger portion of the Spirit's help,
that each may offer the sacrifice of praise to God. If we
offer glory to God *in* the Spirit, we mean that the Spirit
enables us to fulfill the requirements of true religion. According to this usage, then, we say we are *in* the Spirit,
but it is not objectionable for someone to testify, "the
Spirit of God is *in* me, and I offer glory because His grace
has given me the wisdom to do so." The words of Paul
are appropriate: "I think that I have the Spirit of God," [325]
and "guard the truth that has been entrusted to you by
the Holy Spirit who dwells with*in* us." [326] Likewise it is said,

---

[325] I Cor. 7:40.   [326] II Tim. 1:14.

concerning Daniel: "the Holy Spirit of God is in you." [327]
Men of similar virtue may be described in the same way.

64. We do not deny that something else can be understood from this manner of saying the doxology. We learn that just as the Father is made visible *in* the Son, so also the Son is recognized *in* the Spirit. To worship *in* the Spirit implies that our intelligence has been enlightened. Consider the words spoken to the Samaritan woman. She was deceived by local custom into believing that worship could only be offered in a specific place, but the Lord, attempting to correct her, said that worship ought to be offered in Spirit and in truth.[328] By *truth* He clearly meant Himself. If we say that worship offered *in* the Son (the Truth) is worship offered *in* the Father's Image, we can say the same about worship offered *in* the Spirit since the Spirit in Himself reveals the divinity of the Lord. The Holy Spirit cannot be divided from the Father and the Son in worship. If you remain outside the Spirit, you cannot worship at all, and if you are *in* Him you cannot separate Him from God. Light cannot be separated from what it makes visible, and it is impossible for you to recognize Christ, the Image of the invisible God, unless the Spirit enlightens you. Once you see the Image, you cannot ignore the light; you see the Light and the Image simultaneously. It is fitting that when we see Christ, the Brightness of God's glory, it is always through the illumination of the Spirit. Through Christ the Image, may we be led to the Father, for He bears the seal of the Father's very likeness.

---

[327] Dan. 4:6, (LXX).   [328] Cf. Jn. 4:24.

CHAPTER 27. *How did the word* with *begin to be used? What is its strength? Also concerning the unwritten laws of the Church.*

65.   Our opponents claim that the word *in* is the most appropriate for the Spirit, since every thought concerning Him is sufficiently expressed by its use. They ask why we have introduced this new phrase "*with* the Spirit" instead of using "*in* the Holy Spirit;" they claim that such an expression is unnecessary, and cannot be found in any ecclesiastical tradition. But I have already proven earlier in this treatise that the word *in* is not unique to the Spirit, but is commonly used for the Father and the Son. Furthermore, I believe I have sufficiently demonstrated that the word *in* detracts nothing from the Spirit's dignity. Not only that; I claim that its use leads everyone to the greatest heights, except those whose minds are poisoned. It remains for me to describe the origin and force of the word "*with*" and to show that its usage is in accord with Scripture.

66.   Concerning the teachings of the Church, whether publicly proclaimed (*kerygma*) or reserved to members of the household of faith (dogmata), we have received some from written sources, while others have been given to us secretly, through apostolic tradition. Both sources have equal force in true religion. No one would deny either source — no one, at any rate, who is even slightly familiar with the ordinances of the Church. If we attacked unwritten customs, claiming them to be of little importance, we would fatally mutilate the Gospel, no matter what our intentions — or rather, we would reduce the Gospel teachings to bare words. For instance (to take the first and most common example), where is the written teaching that we should sign with the sign of the Cross those who, trusting in the Name of Our Lord Jesus Christ, are to be enrolled as catechumens? Which book teaches us to pray facing the East? Have any saints left for us in writing the words to be used in the invocation over the Eucharistic bread and the cup of blessing? As everyone knows, we are not content in the liturgy simply to recite the words recorded by St. Paul or the Gospels, but we add other words both before and after, words of great importance for this mystery. We have received these words from unwritten teaching. We bless baptismal water and the oil for chrismation as well as the candidate approaching the font. By what written authority do we do this, if not from secret and mystical tradition? Even beyond blessing the oil, what written command do we have to anoint with it? What about baptizing a man with three immersions, or other baptismal rites, such as the renunciation of Satan and his angels? Are not all these things found in unpublished and unwritten teachings, which our fathers guarded in silence, safe from meddling and petty curiosity? They had learned their lesson well; reverence for the mysteries is best encouraged by silence. The uninitiated were not even allowed to be present at the mysteries; how could you expect these teachings to be paraded about in public documents? Why did the great Moses not open every part of the meeting-tent to everyone? [329] The unclean he placed outside the sacred precincts, while the first court was assigned for the ritually pure. He judged only the Levites worthy to serve God,[330] while sacrifies, burnt-offerings, and other priestly functions were reserved to the priests.[331] Only one chosen from all the priests was admitted into the innermost sanc-

---

[329] Cf. Num. 4:20.   [330] Num. 18:22ff.   [331] Num. 18:7.

tuary,[332] but only on one day each year. Even on this one day he entered for only a short time, so that he would be amazed by the novelty and strangeness of gazing on the Holy of Holies. Moses was wise enough to realize that triteness and familiarity breed contempt, but the unusual and the unfamiliar naturally commands eager interest. In the same way, when the apostles and Fathers established ordinances for the Church, they protected the dignity of the mysteries with silence and secrecy from the beginning, since what is noised abroad to anyone at random is no mystery at all. We have unwritten tradition so that the knowledge of dogma might not become neglected and scorned through familiarity. Dogma is one thing, kerygma another; the first is observed in silence, while the latter is proclaimed to the world. One form of silence is the obscurity found in certain passages of Scripture, which makes the meaning of some dogmas difficult to perceive for the reader's own advantage. For instance, we all pray facing East, but few realize that we do this because we are seeking Paradise, our old fatherland, which God planted in the East in Eden.[333] We all stand for prayer on Sunday, but not everyone knows why. We stand for prayer on the day of the Resurrection to remind ourselves of the graces we have been given: not only because we have been raised with Christ and are obliged to seek the things that are above,[334] but also because Sunday seems to be an image of the age to come. Notice that although Sunday is the beginning of days, Moses does not call it the *first* day, but *one* day: "And there was evening and there was morning, one day," [335] since this day would recur many times. Therefore "one" and "eight" are the same, and the "one" day really refers both to itself and to the "eighth" day. Even the Psalmist follows this usage in certain titles of the

---

[332] Ex. 30:10; Lev. 16:2.   [334] Col. 3:1.
[333] Gen. 2:8.   [335] Gen. 1:5.

psalms.[336] This day foreshadows the state which is to follow the present age: a day without sunset, nightfall, or successor, an age which does not grow old or come to an end. It is therefore necessary for the Church to teach her newborn children to stand for prayer on this day, so that they will always be reminded of eternal life, and not neglect preparations for their journey. The entire season of Pentecost is likewise a reminder of the resurrection we expect in the age to come. If we count that one day, the first of days, and then multiply it seven times seven, we will have completed the seven weeks of the holy Pentecost, and the season ends on the same day it began (Sunday) with fifty days having elapsed. Therefore this season is an image of eternity, since it begins and ends at the same point, like a circle. During this time the ordinances of the Church instruct us to pray standing, and by this reminder our minds are made to focus on the future instead of the present. Also, every time we bend our knees for prayer and then rise again, we show by this action that through sin we fell down to earth, but our Creator, the Lover of Mankind, has called us back to heaven.

67. Time would fail me if I attempted to list all the unwritten mysteries of the Church, so I will not mention any others, except this: in which writings do we find our confession of faith in Father, Son, and Holy Spirit? If we are obliged to believe in that into which we have been baptized, then we must make our confession of faith in the same terms as our baptism. Since we have received those terms from the baptismal tradition, let our opponents follow the principles of true religion, and allow us to glorify God with the same terms we use to profess our faith. If they refuse to accept our doxology because we have no written authorization for it, let them

---

[336] Cf. Ps. 6 and 12, (LXX).

give us written evidence for the profession of faith and the other practices we have enumerated. Since there are so many unwritten traditions, having great importance in the mystery of true religion, how can they refuse to concede to us the use of a single word, which has come to us from the Fathers — a word we discovered to have remained in use in unperverted churches, unintentionally transmitted by custom? Can they not see that the arguments for this word are strong and that its contribution to the power of the mystery is by no means small?

68. I have explained the force of both expressions. Now I shall again describe their similarities and differences in usage. They are not antagonistic expressions; it is simply that each has a unique meaning, as far as true religion is concerned. The preposition *in* expresses the relationship between ourselves and the Spirit, while *with* proclaims the communion of the Spirit with God. Therefore we use both words: the latter expresses the Spirit's dignity, while the former describes the grace we have been given. We glorify God both in the Spirit and with the Spirit; we have not invented this word, but we follow the teaching of the Lord as our rule, and transfer this word to things which are logically related, sharing a common mystery: He is numbered *with* Them in the baptismal formula, and we consider it necessary to combine Their Names in the same way when we profess our faith, and we treat the profession of faith as the origin and mother of the doxology. What can they do now? Either they must teach us not to baptize in the manner we have been taught, or else not to believe as we were baptized, or not to glorify as we believe. Can anyone deny that the sequence of relationship in these acts must necessarily remain unbroken? Will anyone deny that innovation here will mean disaster everywhere? Still they continue screaming in our ears that to give glory *with* the Holy Spirit is unauthorized, unscriptural, et cetera. We have already said that as far as our understanding is concerned, to say "Glory to the Father *and* to the Son *and* to the Holy Spirit" means the same as "Glory to the Father *and* to the Son *with* the Holy Spirit." We have received the word *and* from the very words of the Lord, and no one would dare to deny or cancel it, so what could possibly hinder our acceptance of its equivalent? We have already shown the similarities and differences between the two words. Our argument is confirmed by the fact that the Apostle uses both words indifferently: he says in one place "in the name of our Lord Jesus Christ *and* in the Spirit of our God," [337] and in another, "When you are assembled and my Spirit is present, *with* the power of our Lord Jesus." [338] He obviously has no idea that using the conjunction or the preposition affects the combination of names in any way.

CHAPTER 28. *Although Scripture describes men as reigning together* with *Christ, our opponents will not allow this word to be used concerning the Spirit.*

69. Let us see if we can think of any defense for our fathers' use of this word, since those who started the expression are more at fault than we ourselves. Paul says in the Epistle to the Colossians: "And you, who were dead in your sins and the uncircumcision of your flesh, God made alive together with Christ." [339] Did God give to the Church and to an entire race the gift of life with Christ,

---

[337] I Cor. 6:11.   [338] I Cor. 5:4.   [339] Col. 2:13.

if the life with Christ has nothing to do with the Holy
Spirit? If it is impious to even think such a thing, is it not
reverent to confess our faith in those who are closely
united by nature? What a boundless lack of common
sense! These men confess that the saints are with Christ
(since Paul most assuredly says that he would rather be
away from the body and at home with Christ,[340] and that
his desire is to depart and be with Christ,) [341] yet they
dare refuse the Spirit even the communion that Christ
shares with men! Paul calls himself a fellow-laborer with
God in the administration of the Gospel; [342] will they then
indict us for blasphemy if we also call the Spirit a fellow-
laborer, since through Him the Gospel bears fruit in every
creature under heaven? It seems to me that if the life of
those who have trusted in the Lord is hidden with Christ
in God, and when Christ, Who is their life appears, then
they also will appear with Him in glory,[343] how then could
the Spirit of life, who has set us free from the law of sin [344]
not be with Christ, whether in the secret and hidden life
of God, or in the manifestation of the glory which we
expect to be revealed in the saints? We are heirs of God
and fellow heirs with Christ,[345] yet does the Spirit have
no inheritance or portion in the fellowship of God and
His Christ? "It is the Spirit Himself bearing witness with
our spirit that we are children of God;" [346] will we deprive
the Spirit of His testimony of fellowship with God, which
the Lord has taught us? Truly this is the height of folly:
if we, through faith in Christ which we can only confess
in the Spirit, hope that we shall be raised up and sit together with Christ in the heavenly places,[347] and that He
will change our lowly body from the natural to the spiri-

---

[340] II Cor. 5:8.   [343] Cf. Col. 3:3-4.   [346] Rom. 8:16.
[341] Phil. 1:23.   [344] Cf. Rom. 8:2.   [347] Eph. 2:6.
[342] Cf. I Cor. 3:9.   [345] Rom. 8:17.

tual,[348] how can we refuse to allow the Spirit any share in
this enthronement, or glory, or anything else we have received from Him! We believe ourselves to have been made
worthy of many gifts through Christ's sure promise; are we
to permit the Holy Spirit to have none of them, as if He
was beneath their dignity? It is your privilege to be always
with the Lord; you expect to be "caught up in the clouds
to meet the Lord in the air, and to always be with the
Lord"; [349] how can you deny that the Spirit is *with* Christ
and declare the man who numbers and ranks the Spirit
with the Father and the Son as guilty of unbearable
impiety?

70. I am ashamed even to write what follows. You
expect to be glorified together with Christ (provided we
suffer with Him in order that we may also be glorified
with Him),[350] yet you refuse to glorify the Spirit of holiness
together with Christ, as though He is not even worthy to
share the same glory as you. You hope to reign with Christ,
but you insult the Spirit of grace, because you assign Him
the rank of a slave or a subordinate. I am not saying that
the Spirit deserves only the same glory we hope to receive,
but I am trying to shame those who are unwilling to give
Him even this, and shrink from the Spirit's communion of
glory with Son and Father as if it were blasphemy. Who
can speak of there things without sighing? It is not obvious
even to someone with a child's intelligence that the present state of affairs is only the beginning of an impending
eclipse of the faith? What was once undeniable is now
attacked on every side. We profess faith in the Spirit, and
then quarrel with our own creed. We are baptized and
begin fighting again. We call upon the Spirit as the Prince
of Life, and then despise Him as a slave like ourselves.
We received Him with Father and Son, yet we dishonor

---

[348] Cf. Phil. 3:21; I Cor. 15:44. [349] I Thess. 4:17. [350] Rom. 8:17.

Him, calling Him a part of creation. We do not know how to pray as we should,[351] and are not capable of uttering a single word worthy of the Spirit, yet these men attempt to cut Him down to their own size with carefully constructed phrases. They should bewail their own wretchedness instead, and realize that we are all powerless to sufficiently express in words the graces with which we have been filled. He passes all understanding, and exposes the natural inability of our speech to even remotely approach His dignity, as it is written in the Book of Wisdom: "Exalt Him as much as you can, for He is above all praise. When you exalt Him put forth all your strength, and be not weary, for you can never go far enough."[352] How fearful will be the account you will have to give for your words to the God who cannot lie, who said that blasphemy against the Holy Spirit will never be forgiven?[353]

CHAPTER 29. *Enumeration of well-known men in the Church who have used the word* with *in their writings.*

71. The objection is that there is no written authority for the doxology in the form "with the Spirit" but this is valid only if no other unwritten traditions can be found. However, if many of our mysteries have been handed down from unwritten sources, then let us receive this one with all the rest. It is in the apostolic spirit to follow unwritten traditions, as St. Paul says: "I commend you because you remember me in everything and maintain the traditions even as I have delivered them to you,"[354] or "stand firm

[351] Rom. 8:26. [353] Lk. 12:10.
[352] Sir. 43:33-34. [354] I Cor. 11:2.

and hold to the traditions which you were taught by us either by word of mouth or by letter." [355] One of these traditions is in question now, although those who started it passed it on to their successors, and it has become firmly established in the Churches through long custom. Its use has increased with the passage of time. If I were on trial, with no written evidence for my defense, could you not be persuaded to vote for my acquittal if I produced a crowd of witnesses? I think so, since "by the evidence of two or three witnesses shall a charge be sustained." [356] In addition to this, if my witnesses' testimony covered a long period of time, would I not have suitably proven to you that the charge should not have been brought against me? Likewise, we are compelled to accept old teachings, since their hoary antiquity inspires reverence. Therefore I will list for you those who have supported this word (the span of time covered by these men must certainly be taken into account and will justify our passing by many of them in silence). We were not the first to use this word. How could we be? Compared to the length of time this word has been used, our own span of years, as Job says, is but of yesterday.[357] Speaking for myself, I inherited the use of this word from the fathers. It was entrusted to me by a man who had spent many years in God's service; I was both baptized and ordained to serve the Church by him. As I examined, as far as I was able, whether any of the blessed men of old had used these words which are now contested, I found many who are noteworthy for their early date and also — certainly unlike men today — for the precision of their knowledge. Some of them joined the Names in the doxology with the preposition and others with the conjunction, but none of them are at variance — at least concerning what true religion really has to say about this question.

---

[355] II Thess. 2:15.   [356] Deut. 19:15.   [357] Job. 8:9.

72. There is Irenaeus and Clement of Rome, and
Dionysius of Rome, and Dionysius of Alexandria, who,
strangely enough, concludes his second letter to his name-
sake "On Accusation and Defense" as follows. I will quote
his very words for you: "Since we have received a form
and a rule from the presbyters who have gone before us,
we offer thanksgiving in harmony with them, and following everything they have taught us, we conclude our letter
to you. To God the Father, and the Son Our Lord Jesus
Christ, *with* the Holy Spirit be glory and dominion unto
ages of ages. Amen." No one can claim that someone has
tampered with this passage: the use of the phrase "in
the Spirit" is far more common, yet notice that he uses
"with the Spirit" here, and as his defense he continually
insists that he conforms to a form and a rule already received. The same Dionysius writes in the middle of his
treatise against the Sabellians: "Though they claim that
the idea of three persons divides the Godhead, nevertheless there are three, whether they like it or not. Otherwise they would completely destroy the divine Trinity."
Again he says, "After we recognize the Unity, we must
then consider the most divine Trinity." Clement, who
wrote much earlier, says: "God lives, and the Lord Jesus
Christ, and the Holy Spirit." [858] But now let us hear how
Irenaeus, who lived close to apostolic times, wrote concerning the Spirit in his book against heresies: "The
Apostle rightly calls carnal those who are unbridled and
are carried away by their own lusts, having no desire for
the Holy Spirit." In another passage he says: "Let us
beware that having no share in the divine Spirit, we fail
to obtain the heavenly kingdom, since the Apostle said:
'flesh and blood cannot inherit the kingdom of God.' " For
those who accept the authority of Eusebius of Caesarea
on account of his extensive history, allow me to refer to

---

[858] I Clem. 58.

his discussion of polygamy among the ancients. In his preface to this work he invokes "the holy God of the prophets, the Giver of Light, through our Savior Jesus Christ, *with* the Holy Spirit."

73. We find Origen using the form of the doxology "with the Holy Spirit" in many of his commentaries on the psalms. His notions concerning the Spirit are not always sound, but in many passages he recognizes the force of long-established usage, and his words are consonant with true religion. In the sixth book of his *Commentary on the Gospel according to John*, if I am not mistaken,[359] he clearly declares that the Holy Spirit is to be worshipped, using these words: "The washing with water is a symbol of spiritual cleansing, when the filth of wickedness is washed away from the soul. Nevertheless, if a man submits himself to the Godhead of the adorable Trinity, this washing will become the source and the fountain of graces for him, through the power of the invocation (epiclesis). Again, in his commentary on the Epistle to the Romans, he says: "The holy powers are able to reflect the Only-Begotten, and the divinity of the Holy Spirit." See how the powerful force of tradition often compels men to express themselves in terms contrary to their own opinions. This form of the doxology was familiar even to Africanus the historian. In the fifth book of his history he says: "We who are acquainted with the meaning of prophecy, and are not ignorant of the grace of faith, offer thanks to the Father, who gave Jesus Christ, the Savior of all and our Lord, to us, His own creatures. Glory and majesty be to Him, with the Holy Spirit, unto all ages." There are other passages of dubious authenticity but whether they have been altered or not is difficult to tell, since the difference consists of only a single syllable.

---

[359] Actually he is mistaken; it is the eighth book.

However, my extensive quotes can be verified from the actual texts, and are safe from any dishonest manipulation. Now some might say that my next piece of evidence is petty, but since I am accused of introducing novelties, I cannot omit it, because of its great antiquity: Our fathers thought that they should welcome the gift of evening light with something better than silence, so they gave thanks as soon as it appeared. We cannot say who composed these words of thanksgiving at the lighting of the lamps, but the people use these ancient words, and no one accuses them of blasphemy for singing "We praise Father, Son, and God's Holy Spirit." If you are familiar with the hymn of Athenogenes,[360] which he left as a gift to his disciples as he went to his martyrdom by fire, then you know what the martyrs think concerning the Spirit. But of this I have said enough.

74.   Where shall we rank Gregory the Great and his words?[361] Shall we not number with the apostles and prophets a man who walked in the same Spirit? He never strayed from the footsepts of the saints for a day in his life; he strictly fulfilled the duties of the Gospel without wavering. I say this: we sin against the truth if we do not number that soul in the household of God, since he shines as a radiant beacon in the Church of God. He cooperated with the Spirit and was given fearful power over demons; he received such grace for preaching "the obedience of faith among all the nations," [362] that although when he arrived in Pontus he found only seventeen Christians, he soon brought all the people, whether in town or country, to the

---

[360] Traditionally the Vesper hymn of the Byzantine rite: Φῶς ἱλαρὸν or "O Gladsome Light."

[361] Gregory the Wonderworker, bishop of Neocaesarea, disciple of Origen.

[362] Rom. 1:3.

knowledge of God. By Christ's mighty Name he even commanded rivers to change their courses and once when some brothers were quarreling over a lake, each wishing to possess it for his own, he caused it to dry up. His predictions of future things were no less than those of the other prophets. To describe all his miracles in detail would take too long; by the working of the Spirit he was filled with a superabundance of grace, which manifested itself in such powerful signs and wonders that he was called a second Moses even by the enemies of the Church. A light seemed to shine in everything he accomplished through grace, whether by word or deed, reminding everyone of the invisible heavenly power which accompanied him. To this very day he is a source of great wonder to his countrymen, and his memory has not grown old with time, remaining as fresh in the churches as the green of spring. There has not been added a single practice, word, or sacramental rite to those he established for his church; in fact, they follow such a primitive usage that outsiders often think their services are incomplete. His successors permit no innovations, but administer the Churches in exactly the same way he did. Now one of Gregory's institutions is the doxology in the manner now contested, and his church preserves this usage as a tradition received from him; if you insist on proof, all you need do is make a short journey and hear it yourselves. My own predecessor Firmilian used this doxology; you can find it in his writings, and Meletius' contemporaries say that he most assuredly used it as well. But why continue quoting ancient sources? Is not this one word a password in our own day, by which those who hold the true religion may be distinguished from those who do not? I once heard a certain Mesopotamian, a man experienced both in language and accurate knowledge, say that in his country it is not possible to say the doxology in any other way, even if one wishes to do so, since the grammatical rules of their language force them to use their equivalent of the conjunction "and." Our Cappadocian dialect is similar; perhaps the Spirit foresaw how useful this word would be, when he gave the gift of tongues to the disciples! What about the entire West, almost from Illyricum to the boundaries of the empire? Does it not prefer this word?

75. How can I be an innovator, or a creator of new words, when I have listed as originators and champions of this word entire peoples and cities, custom older than any-one's memory, men who were pillars of the Church, distin-guished in all knowledge, filled with the Spirit's power? Despite all this, an array of enemies fights against us, and every city and village is full of slanderers, even in the re-motest regions. These things cause sadness and pain for hearts that seek after peace, but those who patiently en-dure suffering for the faith will be greatly rewarded. Besides all this, then, let the sword flash, let the axe be sharpened, let the fire burn fiercer than the furnace in Babylon, let every instrument of torture be set against us. For me, nothing is more fearful than failing to fear the Lord's threats against those who blaspheme the Spirit. Prudent readers will find in my words a satisfactory de-fense: I accept a word that is familiar and dear to the saints, confirmed by long usage. From the day when the Gospel was first preached even until now, it has been welcomed by the churches, and, most important of all, has been defined in conformity to righteousness and true religion. And what have we prepared for our defense on the great day of judgment? I will say that we were led to glorify the Spirit because the Lord Himself first honored Him; He associated the Spirit with Himself and the Father when He gave us the baptismal formula. Secondly, it was through this very initiation that we were introduced to the knowledge of God. But most of all, it was the threat of punishment which kept us away from unworthy definitions and demeaning opinions. As for our opponents, what will they have to say? What defense will they have for their blasphemy? They have neither shown reverence to the honor which the Lord paid to the Spirit, nor have they feared His threats. They are responsible for their own actions; they can change their minds if they wish. For my own part, I fervertly pray that the good God will make His peace to reign in everyone's heart, so that these men who are swollen with pride and who bitterly rage against us may be calmed by the Spirit of gentleness and love. But if they become utterly wild, may the Lord enable us to at least endure with patience everything we must suffer at their hands. At any rate, suffering for the faith is not painful for those who already bear in themselves the sentence of death; rather, it is our impatience to fight the battle that is difficult. An athlete does not complain much about getting wounded in the contest, but he would be in agony if he were not even admitted into the stadium. But perhaps this is a time for silence, as wise Solomon wrote in Ecclesiastes. When life is tossed about by so violent a storm that the minds of everyone instructed in the word have been thrown into confusion and filled with the deceit of false reasoning, like an eye blinded by sand, when everyone is stunned by strange and terrible noises, when all the world is shaken and everything tottering to its fall, what use is it to cry to the wind?

CHAPTER 30. *Description of the present conditions of the Churches.*

76. To what can I compare our present condition? It is like a naval battle, kindled by old quarrels, fought by men who love war, who cultivate hatred for one another,

and have long experience in naval warfare. Look at the
fearful picture I am painting for you; see the rival fleets
rushing against each other on both sides, and finally they
converge in a burst of desperate fury. Imagine, if you
will, the ships driven into confusion by a raging tempest,
while thick darkness falls from the clouds and blackens
the entire scene, so that signals cannot be recognized, and
one can no longer distinguish between friend and foe. To
add more details to this picture, imagine the sea swollen
and whirling up from the deeps, while torrents of rain pour
from the clouds and the terrible waves rise higher and
higher. All four winds meet together and dash one fleet
against the other. Meanwhile some of the combatants are
betraying each other; some are deserting in the middle of
the battle; while others at the same time are compelled,
while the wind drives them on, to urge their boats forward
against the enemy. The men become jealous of those in
higher authority, and lusting for power among themselves,
they split into factions and begin to slaughter each other.
Think of the confused and unintelligible din raging over
the entire sea, from the howling winds, the splintering of
ships, the boiling surf, the cries of the warriors as they
give vent to their passions with every kind of noise, so
that not a single word from the admiral or pilot can be
heard. The disorder and confusion is beyond description,
but the worst evil of all soon raises its head: once men
despair for their lives, they claim license for every sort
of wickedness. Suppose they are stricken with the incurable sickness of megalomania; then they will not cease their
efforts to defeat one another even as their ships sink into
the abyss.

77. Now I ask you to turn from this fanciful description to the evil reality. When the Arian schism was
first denounced as a sect opposed to the Church of God,
did it not appear then to stand alone? But when the

enemy's policy against us was changed from one of long and bitter contention to open warfare, then, as everyone knows, the war was split into a myriad of factions, so that all men succumbed to irreconcilable hatred, either through individual suspicion or party spirit. What storm at sea was ever so savage as this tempest of the Churches? It has moved every boundary established by the Fathers; every foundation, every established bulwark of doctrine has been shaken. Everything still remaining afloat is shaken by unsound teaching and thrown back into the abyss. We attack one another; we are overthrown by one another. If the enemy does not strike us first we are wounded by our comrade; if he is wounded and falls, he is trampled by his fellow soldier. Although we are united in our hatred of common foes, no sooner do they retreat, and we find enemies in each other. Who could even list all the casualties? Some have fallen in battle with the enemy; some have been treacherously betrayed by their allies; others are the victims of their leaders' incompetence. Entire churches are dashed and shattered on the sunken reefs of subtle heresy, while other enemies of the Spirit of salvation have seized the helm and made shipwreck of the faith. The tumults devised by the princes of this world have brought about the downfall of the people with violence surpassing hurricane or tornado. A darkness full of gloom and misery has descended on the Churches: the lights of the world, established by God to enlighten the souls of the people, have been exiled.[363] The terror of universal destruction already hangs over us, yet they continue enjoying their rivalries, ignoring any sense of danger. Private enmities are more important to these men that the struggle of an entire people; they prefer the glory of subduing their opponents to securing the common welfare,

---

[363] St. Basil refers to the many bishops exiled under emperor Valens.

and they love the immediate delights of worldly honor more than the rewards awaiting us in the age to come. So all men alike, depending on how much power each one has, rush upon each other with murderous hands. They fight against each other with harsh words; they nearly fill the Church with the meaningless cries and unintelligible shouts of their incessant clamor. They continually pervert the teachings of true religion, sometimes by adding to them, and other times by reducing them. On the one hand are those who confuse the Persons and revert to Judaism; on the other are those who oppose the natures, and are swept away into Greek polytheism. Inspired scripture is powerless to mediate between these two parties, nor can apostolic tradition offer them terms of reconciliation. One honest word and your friendship with them is finished; one disagreement with their opinions is sufficient pretext for a quarrel. No oath is so effective for holding a conspiracy together as common fellowship in error. Every man is a theologian; it does not matter that his soul is covered with more blemishes than can be counted. The result is that these innovators find an abundance of men to join their factions. So ambitious, self-elected men divide the government of the Churches among themselves, and reject the authority of the Holy Spirit. The ordinances of the Gospel have been thrown into confusion everywhere for lack of discipline; the jostling for high positions is incredible, as every ambitious man tries to thrust himself into high office. The result of this lust for power is that wild anarchy prevails among the people; the exhortations of those in authority are rendered utterly void and unprofitable, since every man in his arrogant delusion thinks that it is more his business to give orders to others than to obey anyone himself.

78. Since no human voice is powerful enough to be heard in such an uproar, I reckon that silence is more profitable than words. If the words of the Preacher are true: "The words of the wise are heard in quiet," [364] then with the present state of affairs, any discussion of them at all is scarcely appropriate. Moreover, I am restrained by the prophet's words: "Therefore he who is prudent will keep silent in such a time; for it is an evil time," [365] a time when some trip their neighbors, others kick a man already fallen, others applaud, but no one is sympathetic enough to lend a helping hand to the weary, even though the old law says "if you see the beast of one who hates you lying under its burden, you shall refrain from leaving him with it, but you shall help him to lift it up." [366] This is certainly not the case now. Why not? The love of many has grown cold; concord among brothers is no more; the very name of unity is ignored; Christian compassion or sympathetic tears cannot be found anywhere. There is no one to welcome someone weak in faith,[367] but mutual hatred blazes so fiercely among brothers that a neighbors' fall brings them more joy than their own household's success. And just as a contagious disease spreads from the sick to the healthy during an epidemic, in these days we have become like everyone else: imitators of evil, carried away by this wicked rivalry possessing our souls. Those who judge the erring are merciless and bitter, while those judging the upright are unfair and hostile. This evil is so firmly rooted in us that we have become more brutish than the beasts: At least they herd together with their own kindred, but we reserve our most savage warfare for the members of our own household.

79.   These are the reasons I should have kept quiet, but love pulled me in the opposite direction, the love that is not self-seeking,[368] but desires to conquer every obstacle

---

[364] Eccl. 9:17.   [366] Ex. 23:5.   [368] Cf. I Cor. 13:5.
[365] Amos 5:13.   [367] Rom. 14:1.

put in her way by time and circumstance. I learned from the example of the children in Babylon that when there is no one to support the cause of true religion, we must accomplish our duties alone. They sang a hymn to God from the midst of the flames, not thinking of the multitudes who rejected the truth, but content to have each other, though there were only three of them. Therefore the cloud of our enemies does not dismay us, but we place our trust in the Spirit's help, and boldly proclaim the truth. Otherwise, it would be utterly miserable that the Spirit is blasphemed and true religion is wrecked so easily by these men, while we, having such a mighty patron and protector, hesitate to defend a doctrine which has been maintained in unbroken sequence from the days of the fathers until now. The fervor of your sincere love and your quiet, serious disposition, also provided me with powerful encouragement. I know that you will refrain from divulging my words to all the world to see; not that they are not worth hearing, but to avoid casting pearls before swine. Now my task is finished. If you find that what I have said is satisfactory, let it end our discussion of these matters. If anything is unclear, do not hesitate to diligently seek an answer; you will add to your knowledge by asking questions while avoiding strife. Either through me or through others the Lord will provide a full answer for any remaining questions, since He gives knowledge to those He has chosen, by the Holy Spirit.